Don't Be A Dick

ISBN: 978-1-63950-049-9   [Paperback Edition]
        978-1-63950-050-5   [eBook Edition]

Printed and bound in The United States of America.

Writers Apex

Gateway Towards Success

8063 MADISON AVE #1252
Indianapolis, IN 46227
+13176596889

www.writersapex.com

DON'T BE A
DICK

The Key to Effective Communication

•••

JASON MENARD

*For my wife who believes she is the funny one
and my daughter who has no clue how hilarious she really is.*

Je t'aime

FORWARD

"Now, a great man once said,
that some people rob you with a fountain pen."
— Bob Dylan

I'm going to be blunt right from the start. We all know someone who needs "Don't Be A Dick" tattooed inside their eyelids. If some of you are honest enough it might just be you! They say it takes all kinds to make the world go round and unfortunately even dicks are part of that tired cliché.

The title of Jason's book alone should be enough. Can't be much more clear on how to talk to and treat other people. Maybe even leave it displayed, cover up on the coffee table when company comes over as a quick reminder before all the conversations start. Some workplaces could even use it on the boardroom table.

What I like most about what Jason has done here is present an honest look at behaviours he's observed over time and adds anecdotes about his marriage, work and social encounters. He's talking "to" and not "at" us. He makes it clear that he's no expert but eloquently covers many types of people we all encounter, live with or work with. Some sections for you will feel like he's peering directly into your soul, you see so much of yourself.

In a sea of self-proclaimed "experts" this blunt and humorous observational read, let's everyone take away something different. You'll

1

learn how to identify different ways your family, friends colleagues and acquaintances communicate for better or worse.

As a morning radio host and standup comic, my entire world relies on rule two of this book. Know your audience. While in radio, my audience for the most part stays the same. In comedy, each crowd is different and I need to pivot quick if I notice I misread the room. The same applies to day-to-day dealings and this book will help you navigate how everyone around you communicates.

Enjoy the ride and I apologize in advance for Jason if, by the time you're done, you realize you are, in fact, a dick.

PREFACE

"Comedy is simply a funny way of being serious"
— Peter Ustiov

Why don't be a dick? The reason I have decided to write this book is because I wanted to shed some light and humour on a harsh reality: people have lost the ability to be effective communicators. There is a surplus of dicks in our society and it is only getting worse.

Self-help books are a dime a dozen. We are drowning in a sea of them, and they are currently invading bookstore shelves and flooding the internet. It seems everyone is an expert on giving advice.

I am not an expert. The following pages contain my opinions regarding this growing epidemic. These opinions are based on my own personal experiences and not on research or facts. Instead of psychobabble, I offer just my views, my beliefs and a concept I have adopted in my everyday life.

I will be categorizing behaviours that take away from conversations and inhibit communication. I believe in removing these barriers, as they are key elements responsible for communication breakdowns.

My goal is to make you laugh while bringing awareness to some of the behaviours we are guilty of during everyday interactions.

AUTHOR'S CREDENTIALS

"I have an unfortunate personality."
— Orson Welles

As previously mentioned, I am not an expert. I do not claim to be a smart man. I am not a scholar with a series of letters following my name. In fact, I am hardly an educated man. I am a dyslexic college graduate who has been working as a social service worker since 2005.

Since that time, I have worked with troubled youth involved with the law, often in collaboration with local school boards. I even worked briefly in a young offender correctional facility before moving into my current position where I work with teens and adults afflicted with a serious mental illness. In my capacity as an Intensive Case Manager in the mental health field, I continue to work closely with the justice system.

I consider myself to be competent and I am comfortable with my skills but by no means do I consider myself to be an expert. I get irritated with self-proclaimed experts and gurus who offer advice like they are tic-tacs. I believe the best weapons in my arsenal are my listening skills and my ability to be assertive. The art of communication is the strongest asset and the most useful tool I can possess in my trade.

I always find it fascinating to gauge people's reaction when they find out about my job. Many people can't picture me in the helping field. Often, my colleagues and I will get praised because of the population we serve. With very little information or insight, other than knowing which agency signs our paycheck, people will jump to the conclusion that we are selfless, noble or honorable individuals. As if they know anything about us! Although, they wouldn't be entirely wrong. I believe my colleagues have these qualities in spades, yet despite my skills and qualities, I am the first to describe myself as an asshole. It is a source of pride for me to be described as so. I am sure many clients, coworkers and community partners would agree with that statement. I say it like it is and often express what people are thinking but perhaps are too afraid (or too smart) to say. I am an *asshole* but not a dick. This distinction cannot be overemphasized. Knowing these discrepancies are the credentials I wear in writing this book.

DON'T BE A JERK

*"Comedy is the art of making people laugh
without making them puke."*
— ***Steve Martin***

The core concept behind this book started when a colleague and I were appointed to a new file. The referring source had indicated that this individual had a history of aggressive behaviour and was recently charged with assault causing bodily harm. Since he scored high on our violent risk assessment, our supervisor asked us to pair up when attending the client's residence.

Intending to offer case management services, we journeyed together to meet this individual only to be denied access to his motel room. Week after week, we attended his place, only to hear him shouting profanities through his door. Sometimes he would peek through the curtains as he cursed and berated us. I kept thinking this guy was being a jerk while we were trying to help him. Relentlessly, we continued to travel to his motel room, refusing to give up on this man. Despite being denied entry and treated poorly, we would continue to try to reach this guy. After all, we believed that even someone who acts like a jerk deserved to be helped.

On a cold Tuesday morning, we attended the client's residence. We played rock paper, scissors to determine who would get the brunt of the abuse. My thought process was instinctive. "...good ol' reliable rock ...

nothing beats that." Except paper; paper beats rock, which is what Mark played. In one fluid motion, he pulled his hand away from our juvenile game, and adjusted the radio dial, enjoying his victory while listening to the band Halestorm. Defeated, I got out of the car and spotted the client. He was under the stairwell, shivering while enjoying a cigarette. Before I could make a sound, he looked at me and said, "If it's alright with you, I'd like to be left alone. Please don't come back here anymore, and close my file." He didn't shout or curse; he didn't even raise his voice. His body language never changed. It was a very different approach when I consider his demeanor in our previous encounters. I handed him my business card as well as the card for the 24 hour crisis line. He was advised to contact us if he needed anything and I wished him well.

Shocked and surprised, Mark and I drove away from the motel parking lot and headed out for lunch. We were discussing the client's file and his right to refuse any help. After all, the services we offer are voluntary and participation is not mandatory. It's funny how effective communication can be when you are not acting like a jerk. It's safe to say that this client was communicating the same message to us week after week. Our interpretation of the message was a different story. By removing the "jerk" attitude, all that was left were his words. No tone, no aggression, no behaviour; just his words.

We arrived at our typical Taco Tuesday joint and got in line. I ordered 4 soft shell tacos, refusing guacamole even before Lark (that's the Taco Tuesday girl's name. What a lark!) could ask me. I attempted to place a special order; however the supervisor Chantal informed us that this item was recently removed from the Tuesday menu. Without going into detail, she mentioned that one person ruined it for everyone. Mark said that someone needs to remind that person not to be a jerk. I instinctively responded, "those are words to live by." Mark has three great kids: a daughter and twin boys. They are funny but can be challenging at times. Mark explained he had a standing rule in his home. When any of kids cross the line, they are reminded not to be a jerk. He said it is one of those situations where no other explanation is required. Simply put, don't be a jerk.

We finished our lunch, grabbed some coffee and headed back to work, driving along, with a belly full of tacos and an earful of Bob

7

Dylan. Traffic began to slow down when suddenly we were cut off by a man on an e-bike. Slamming on the brakes, I watched this daredevil dart into my lane and squeeze himself between my vehicle and a Ford Econoline van. I honked on my horn and applied the brakes, as the man maneuvered his vehicle while giving me the finger. I had a faint vision of *Jeff Spicolli* saying "Hey Bud, what's your problem?" (Crowe, 1982). I was decelerating, attempting to not hit the e-bike, but once he disrespected me with his rude gesture I could hear myself quoting Sean Penn in his surfer accent: "You Dick!"

What happened next was pure karmic retribution. The man on the e-bike must have been too pre-occupied by flipping me the bird because he did not see the traffic light had turn red. He also did not see the van coming to a halt. I watched him collide with the van in slow motion. I stifled a laugh and changed lanes. He was not going fast enough to cause a major injury. Once the light turned green and I knew the motorist had only bruised his ego and scratched his ride, I drove away with the widest grin on my face. What a teachable moment. This scene screamed, "that's what happens when you are a dick!" As I was pulling away, I could hear Mr. Dylan on the radio wailing, "How does it feel?" I remember thinking it feels pretty good, Bob.

Not feeling the need to censor myself, that day, "Don't be a Jerk", graduated to "Don't be a Dick". I've since adopted this phrase, developed and defined rules to follow this concept and wrote this book.

RULE 1 – DON'T BE A DICK

*"The greatest problem in communication
is the illusion that it has been accomplished."*
— ***George Bernard Shaw***

It seems like a simple concept to me. Just don't be a dick! Truth is, it's not as simple as it appears. You would be surprised how many people cannot help but act like a dick on a regular basis. There are countless forms of *dickery* which are not limited to the examples I will provide. I have developed categories and sub-categories to help us understand some of the regular things we do when conversing. The key thing I try to remember when having a conversation is if I am not adding to the conversation, then I am taking away from it.

Dr. Dick

If you find yourself always trying to rescue people by offering unsolicited advice, then you may be a dick. The individuals that fall in this category are problem solvers. They have the solution to all of your problems and the answers to all the questions you never asked. These people are focused on resolution without stopping to consider the situation. They appear to be so fixated on the problem and how to fix it that they cannot appreciate the complexities of the problem at hand. They are quick to interrupt so they can offer their suggestions and give their opinions.

My opinion – You are being a dick.

Suggestion – Don't be a dick.

My wife and I had been dating for a little over a year when we moved in together. We shared a small two bedroom apartment in the city. We just got engaged and we were prepared to start our future together. After work we would meet up in our living room to talk about our workdays. To be honest, she would speak about of some of her challenges while I was looking for ways to solve every problem she had.

Sometimes, she would come home seeming discouraged and frustrated with herself. She would describe a work situation while remaining as vague as possible, providing very little details. She would focus more on her feelings and less on the triggering events. As a "fixer," I would jump in, trying to find solutions. I would provide her with advice, telling her what she could or should do to solve her problem. Her problem however, was me. She did not need to find a solution. She wanted to be heard and have her feelings validated. She required a safe place to share her frustrations. I was so focused on her problem that I never provided her with an outlet that would allow her to vent.

My wife is an intelligent, task oriented and successful woman. She operates on facts and logic. She can second guess herself at times and it will reflect in her confidence level. When something crosses over to the emotional realm, she can struggle. She understands that emotions can be irrational, so at times she requires a sounding board. She needs to talk it out and hear herself problem-solve until she finds her own solutions. My presence is strictly ornamental.

When my wife comes to me to vent about work related situations and I attempt to rescue her by offering suggestions and advice, I am assuming she has not done her due diligence. I am taking for granted that she has not explored all of her options or that she has hit a wall in her process. I should not assume when she is venting that she has run out of options or that she is asking for help. It is best to reserve opinions and advice until the end of the conversation or when I am asked. The truth is that I don't know what she has tried because she has not shared that information. She has also ignored all probing I made in an attempt to learn more on the matter. This was not the focus or the goal when she was venting.

My wife and I have often said that we would leave work at the office and not talk shop when we get home. Sometimes however, emotions run hot and it is difficult to leave it behind. I have learned that once my wife comes home from work there is a period of time devoted for debriefing or venting about our day. It is a great way to transition between work and home. We have developed a system where I will ask her if this conversation requires my ears or both my ears and my mouth. She usually lets me know what she needs and I am smart enough to appreciate her method. Often, she will go to our bar fridge and bring me a can of listening juice. That is my cue that she does not need me to talk, just listen. In these instances, the conversation normally ends before the can is empty.

I would like to believe that most advice givers do not believe people are too dumb to problem solve on their own or are unable to handle a particular situation. I think they are genuinely trying to help without understanding that the best way to help sometimes is simply to be present. People try too hard to come up with something to say or to offer guidance. It's amazing how little talking is involved in active listening. Just listen.

Askhole

There are many words which appear in the dictionary with multiple meanings. I believe this would be the case for the word *askhole.* I have asked around and completed a web search until I was satisfied with these three explanations.

1. **A person who asks many stupid pointless obnoxious questions (Urban Dictionary, n.d.).**

This explanation describes the behaviours of a toddler or a person who is almost nagging you with incessant queries. Although this could be an irritating experience, children tend to be innocent with a thirst for knowledge. I remember trying to figure out the intricacies and complexities of the world. I am still trying to do that now. It can be exasperating but I think it's an age appropriate behaviour. Asking what you perceive to be meaningless questions seems to be a natural part of a three year old child's development. It becomes a concern when the behaviour increases and becomes the habit of a 13, 23 or 33 year old. It is our duty to make sure this behaviour does not persist in those individuals. It is our responsibility as adults to prevent children from becoming future *askholes*.

2. **Someone who asks for your opinion or advice but never takes your advice and does the exact opposite of what you suggest (Slang, n.d.).**

This description of the word *askhole* is one that hits home for me. Having a wife that thinks out loud and is constantly verbally bouncing ideas is exhausting. It is particularly grueling and frustrating when she asks direct questions and ignores the answers altogether.

Wife: Which should I wear today, the green top or the black one.

Me: I don't care.

Wife: That's not helpful.

Me: The black one looks great on you but the green one is my favorite. You look good in both of them so you really can't go wrong.

Wife: I'll just wear the purple one.

Me: Well that makes sense.

Clearly, my input was not needed for this conversation; however she led me to believe that it was important for me to weigh in. This used to happen daily in my home and would make me hesitant to answer any questions. I have to admit, it did take the pressure off somewhat since my answers didn't matter anyways. She was just thinking out loud and was trying to include me in the process.

3. **Someone who makes statements but verbalizes them in the form of a question.**

Paraphrasing the priest of our local parish, this third explanation is my favorite. Father Jason Pollick's sermon "The Cowardice of Rhetorical Questions" was adapted from Mark 6: 1-13 and it began on a very clever note.

The Cowardice of Rhetorical Questions (Pollock, 2018)

Ever notice how some people ask questions as statements?

See what I did there?

I made a statement but phrased it as a question. What I actually said was I have noticed that some people ask questions as statements and I am hoping you have too.

It's a harmless little rhetorical trick that draws people into a story. But sometimes, rhetorical questions are far from harmless.

Take the gospel passage for today. Jesus returns to his home town of Nazareth, enters the synagogue and begins teaching. Some of the people in the synagogue take offense at him. They take offense for a number of reasons. Chief amongst them being that Jesus was not a trained rabbi, and yet he was surrounded by disciples and was teaching at the synagogue. He was also a 'local boy' that they had all seen grow up and ply his trade as a carpenter before he embarked on his ministry.

So they begin asking questions.

But the problem is, the questions they ask him are not honest, nor are they ever asked directly to him rather, they are grumbled amongst one another. They are questions meant to blame, shame and diminish.

Let's go over their question and translate what they are actually saying.

"Where did this man get all this? What is this wisdom that has been given to him? What deeds of power are being done by his hands!"

The statement in these 'questions' are pretty obvious. "He is not qualified to teach, he has no training, no credentials, no authority, he is a charlatan."

The next questions they ask are "is it not the carpenter, the son of Mary and the brother of James, and Joses, and Judas and Simon, and are not his sisters here with us?"

The statements are once again pretty clear. "He is a manual labourer, the son of an unwed mother, the nothing from a family of nothings whom we have known our whole lives."

It is also telling that they call him 'son of Mary'. In a patriarchal society like ancient Judaism, one would generally trace lineage to one's father. But of course, the whole town knew that Jesus was not Joseph's child so, they called him the 'son of Mary'. It sounds innocent enough until you realize they are actually trying to diminish Jesus by pointing out that he is a bastard (using the word in the dictionary definition of the term and not the pejorative).

Now, who knows why they reacted like such jerks? Chances are, they were irked at someone who had little or no education expounding on spiritual matters more profoundly that they were capable of. Perhaps they were jealous that Jesus was stealing their spotlight. Maybe they feared for their positions of importance in the community. Maybe they just resented a 'local boy' who had done better than them. Who knows?

Either way, they made a snap decision about Jesus and didn't give him the benefit of the doubt. They just decided that he was not worth listening to and so they began to grumble to other people to undermine him.

How different might this situation have gone, if they just listened to Jesus? How differently would it have gone if they had just asked their questions to Jesus loaded as they were?

And more to the point of my sermon, how differently would this discussion have gone if they had just gone up to Jesus and said "We are angry at you and afraid of you because you are threatening us." There by actually opening a dialogue with Jesus. Real progress could have been made that day.

So are we asking the same questions? Are we asking these questions of ourselves, of each other and even of God?

Questions are great, questions are the way we increase our knowledge. But if we are asking questions to make statements we are just being jerks. In the future, perhaps we can restrict our questions to things of which we are actually seeking answers and restrict our statements to things that will make us, our family, our churches and our workplace and communities better places.

I know not everyone can relate or even appreciate a biblical link but I found this sermon to be absolutely brilliant. It was an eye opening experience for me to reflect upon the passive-aggressive comments I have made and have been subjected to. What a notion: say what you mean, mean what you say.

Objectional Askhole

In my line of work, I deal with many lawyers, be it for the defense or for the Crown Attorney's office. I get many opportunities to watch the spectacle unfold during legal proceedings and I experience vicarious *askhole* statements. While these statements serve a purpose in this particular situation, it always amazes me how lawyers create statements and arguments in the form of a question, knowing full well there is no proper way of answering.

When it comes to the justice system, most people's frame of reference stem from TV shows such as "Suits" or "Law and Order." If you are a little older, then perhaps "Matlock" or "Perry Mason" is your point of reference. We get sucked into theatrical scenes that are grossly exaggerated but make for good television.

One of my favorite words that emerged from the legal lexicon is the term "objection." This protest is used so freely on television and on the silver screen. In reality, Canadian legal proceedings rarely see such exaggerated dramatic displays of protestation. Should a lawyer have an objection towards a point of law or procedure they simply stand up and the court will recognize they have a grievance. A lawyer may object to a comment made by opposing counsel and say it with authority when they fear this information will taint or sway the judge or juror. This dispute is mostly used in a trial setting and seldom bellowed with disdain or a condescending tone.

Many of us seem to be unaware of the legal proceedings leading up to a trial. There are many steps and procedures that need to take place before Hollywood's main event. Of course, while watching a movie or television show these steps take a few days, but in reality, they take months or possibly a year.

I was once assisting a lawyer with a matter. I was asked to provide support while the client appeared in court to make his plea and be sentenced. A joint position was agreed upon during the counsel pre-trial conference. To us laymen, a joint position is where both counsels agree on a suitable sentence. The presiding judge will most likely accept this position unless it is outside of the public interest. In this particular case, the individual stood before a judge and was prepared to enter a plea of guilt. The charges were read out loud in court, but before the clerk could finish reading the first set of allegations the individual yelled "objection."

The judge, looking down from his elevated seat and over his glasses explained that if the client did not agree with the charges he could not proceed with a guilty plea. He seemed panicked because he instantly yelled "withdrawn," making a cut throat motion with his fingers to the clerk. The judge offered a weak smirk while alternating glances between counsels. He remained silent for a moment and then finally broke the silence to adjourn the matter for a judicial pre-trial meeting. I shook my head in disbelief, flabbergasted my client thought this was suitable comportment in court.

As fun as the word "objection" is, "withdrawn" is by far my favorite legal jargon. It is the prototypical tool of the Hollywood lawyer; a true *askhole.* You could imagine the movie scene, panning from a southern backdrop and slowly zooming on the justice building; the camera focusing on the state seal. On one side of the courtroom is the district attorney, sitting at his table shuffling papers. He is a dead ringer for a Colonel Saunders look-alike. On the other side is the defense attorney. He is a sharp dressed bespectacled lawyer with slick back hair and a wispy moustache. Brandishing a pompous air, he makes statements formed as questions while cross-examining a witness. Opposing counsel objecting every time he feels threatened. Other times, the *askhole* knows his line of questioning is inappropriate but wants everyone to hear it anyways, and so he will withdraw his own statement before being challenged.

This type of "withdrawn" is almost used as punctuation; like an exclamation mark. It appears at the end of the statement and accentuates its importance. It is used in court as a dismissal. We are supposed to act like we did not hear the statement and it is not intended to sway us.

Obviously people cannot and do not forget those statements and counsel knows that. If anything, it draws more attention to the information that we are not meant to retain, which is why they use those opportunities for such statements.

In the late 1990's, the Canada Revenue Agency took action against Alfonso Caruana, bringing him to Superior Court in Montreal to challenge his bankruptcy claim. The lawyer for the federal tax agency was Chantal Comtois. She was trying to prove that Mr. Caruana did not pay income tax and had evaded the CRA in the past. During the bankruptcy hearing, Curuana presented himself as a struggling immigrant. Comtois tried to make sense as to how 21 million dollars had passed through his bank account. Annoyed with Caruana's evasive answers she asked straight out in court "are you not the godfather of the Italian mafia?" (Noel & Cedilo, 2010). The judge ordered the question withdrawn from the record.

Withdrawn statement or not, the lawyer knew exactly what she was doing. When she was unable to get the answer she wanted she drew attention to the fact that the accused had ties with La Costa Nostra. Whether on record or not, people don't forget that sort of detail.

My wife enjoys drama television shows and courtroom movies like "A Few Good Men". We always laugh when we hear the term "withdrawn." We love this litigating lingo so much we started using it around the house.

Me: I still can't believe you backed the car into the house.

Wife: You said you wouldn't bag on me about that anymore.

Me: Withdrawn.

Of course, it is as silly and absurd to use it socially as it is used in the courtroom on television.

Wife: You are an ass.

Me: Objection!

Wife: Withdrawn. I meant you are acting like an ass.

Me: Please proceed with caution Mrs. Menard.

It is an unusual and funny statement but I don't see its application in a serious situation. Could you imagine using it to retract a rude and highly disrespectful comment? One time, my wife and I attended a wedding where we overindulged in alcohol and took the shuttle back to the hotel. The next day a hungover couple volunteered to drive us back to our vehicle. We witnessed one of the most comical and disturbing exchange that morning.

Her: What is that sound?

Him: The rim is messed up, that's the reason the tire sounds like that.

Her: The rim? It sounds awful.

Him: Yeah, it's bent.

Her: Why don't you pull over and just go hit it with the tire iron?

Him: (sighing, shaking his head).... Fuck, you are dumb.

That would never work in my relationship. At that moment I was praying for a "withdrawn." I almost screamed it myself from the backseat. But she didn't react. She didn't answer him back or even look in his direction. She just took it. Perhaps she didn't hear him (unlikely), perhaps she was too hungover to argue (likely) or perhaps she was use to this type of communication (bingo!). The behaviour you ignore is the behaviour you allow to repeat (write that down kids). I have since attempted to use the "fuck, you are a dumb" followed by "withdrawn" in social settings, but have had very little success.

Constant Corrector

The *Constant Corrector* is a category reserved for the smart ones. Not the smart asses, that's a different category altogether. These individuals are typically of higher intelligence (or disillusioned people who want others to believe they are intelligent). *Constant Correctors* believe they are communicators however they are among the first people to interrupt you mid-sentence. They are compelled to find a reason to disrupt the flow of the dialogue to make a correction.

Detailed-Oriented Dick

This particular *Constant Corrector* will challenge statements knowing full well the corrections will not change the outcome of the story. They are more focused on the accuracy then the plot.

I was describing a story that took place a few weeks prior to some of the boys. Luc and I were watching the baseball game. The Jays were down 2-0 against the Yankees and Luc was telling me one of his fishing stories. Stifling a yawn, I noticed a girl out of my peripheral vision. She appeared to be interested in the game while she sat on a stool at the bar. We overheard her ask the bartender about whiskey. She ordered a single malt scotch: neat. Can you imagine what Luc did next?

Before I could finish the story, Luc's roommate Andre chimed in to make an amendment. He informed us that "the Jays were in Boston last week. They played New York in the Bronx the week before."

While I appreciate Andre's uncanny identic memory, the adversary of the Toronto Blue Jays and the rivalry of the American League's East Division held very little relevance to this conversation. Clearly, the conversation was geared towards the woman at the bar, watching sports and ordering a fine scotch. Since I was interrupted by a minute detail, the audience did not get to hear the rest of the story.

Spoiler alert – Luc went to talk to her and was rejected harder than Muggsy Bogues[1] would, trying to dunk against Manute Bol. [2]

The Scholar

The *Scholar* may appear pretentious, hindering the flow of conversation by improving the orator's grammar and sentence structure. Since English is not my primary language, and because I am a dummy, I am often subjected to the scholar's criticism. I was raised in a French speaking home and educated in French schools. Knowing the importance of bilingualism for my career, I transferred to an English college. I have since adopted the English language and use it

---

1   Tyrone Curtis "Muggsy" Bogues stands at 5'3". He played 14 seasons as a Point Guard in the NBA. He was the shortest player to ever play professionally.

2   Manute Bol stands at 7'7". He played 10 seasons as a center in the NBA. He is one of the two tallest men to ever play professionally.

predominantly at home and at work. For this reason, I have lost a lot of my French vocabulary. I find myself searching for words when having simple conversations. My brilliant dreams of bilingualism fade away when I realize I am sub-par in both languages and constantly being corrected.

Some *Constant Correctors* have a compulsive need to have other's adapt to their own speaking styles, almost as if their way is the only sensible way to have a dialogue. Other *Constant Correctors* are compelled to make adjustments because inappropriate language irks them.

Brrrring Brrring

Me: Hello...

Joe Random: Can I speak with MJ?

Me: No she is not in right now, can I ask to who I am speaking to?

Joe Random: Joe Random... and shouldn't it be whom?

Me: Whom? Of course. How silly of me? By omitting the letter 'M' you must have been confused. I was inquiring as to what your name was and what the nature of this call was?

Joe Random: I was following up with MJ. We have a new promotion, offering to upgrade her phone service.

Me: Me and my wife will discuss it and call you back.

Joe Random: Don't you mean my wife and I?

Me: Of course I was. I hope you didn't misunderstand me? How embarrassing. It definitely will not be me and my wife calling you back. It will be two different people altogether. Expect a call from my wife and I.

And that ladies and gentlemen is how you don't make a sale.

I have to admit that I am guilty of being a *Constant Corrector* in specific situations. I have a really hard time letting go or ignoring certain turns of phrase. It hurts my ears when I hear people pluralizing the word 'you'. The plural of you is you, not yous, youse, yas or yous guys. You'll often hear me correct people by saying "you should never use yous in a sentence".

Another ear burner for me is the term irregardless. The use of the double negative makes the word redundant. The prefix "ir" and the suffix "less" work against each other, cancelling each other out. Not without any regard!?

The worst part of hearing these two terms is that I often hear many intelligent people, individuals in positions of power like politicians or authority figures, expressing themselves with these nomenclatures.

Let's be honest for a moment. Most of us understand what someone is trying to say without having to make unnecessary adjustments. If clarifications are needed to assist you in understanding, then you could easily ask questions for further explanations without sounding like a know it all. Unless you are a teacher speaking to a student or a parent setting a good example for your kin, there is no reason to interrupt someone and belittle them with a public correction.

The next two examples I will be providing for the *Constant Corrector* act as hybrids. These two styles may stand alone or in combination with either the *Scholar or the Detailed-Oriented Dick.*

Random Fact Guy

This *Constant Corrector* may interrupt a conversation to provide you with a remarkable or extraordinary fact. Inserting a random fact can be an attempt to educate or to correct. Often, weird uncommon facts hold little bearing and provide little to any conversation.

I was at a Christmas party a while back. We were talking about some of the dreadful apartments we all inhabited at one time or another when we moved away from our parents home. I mentioned one of the worst places I had rented. It was a miniscule, damp two-bedroom apartment from a very questionable landlord. It was one of the worst place I had ever rented. The door was warped so bad you had to slam it shut every time and lock it to prevent it from randomly popping open. The kitchenette was the size of a closet and it was carpeted.

During the first week I had spotted a cockroach on the counter. I trapped the unholy creature with a rocks glass and held it captive until my roommate was able to get our slumlord to attend our place. He walked into our kitchen and did not appear surprised by the confined insect. He actually said "it's only one bug," to which I replied "one bug!? It's a goddamn roach. A bug! You ever see just one bug?" That was the last comment I made on the subject. My buddy Jack, who was not part of the original conversation had wandered in mid-way and jumped in to inform everyone.

"The Spider Assassin"

He said it without batting an eye. It was said so matter of fact, as if we all knew what he was talking about. There were ten pairs of eyes looking at him in a quizzical way.

"It is also known as the Pelican Spider."

As if this new information provided any sort of clarity. We continued to stare, dumfounded.

"The Spider Assassin originated from Europe, but it is commonly found in South Africa, Madagascar and Australia. They have elongated jaws and necks, perfect for catching insects, especially other spiders. They are considered solitary bugs. So, yeah, sometimes there is only one bug."

I just looked at him, my jaw dropped wide open. Well thank you for that. Who was this guy, Steve Irwin? His words lobotomized me. I stood there speechless. Jack is not a malicious man by any means. He just lacks social awareness at times. Even though his queer interjection in the Tale of the Roach Motel brought the story to a halt, he actually thought he was adding by providing his unusual factoid.

The Actual Technician

This assiduous know-it-all is easy to identify. They begin their correction with the word 'actually' or 'technically'. There is nothing that makes me cringe more than being interrupted, only to hear those words. It is very common amongst millennials. They are letting you know with one word that you need to be corrected and they will be the person to provide you with the proper education.

Actual Technician: Do you want some peanuts?

Joe Random: No thanks, I am allergic to nuts.

Actual Technician: Technically, since the peanut grows underground it is considered a legume and not a nut.

What is the purpose of this added information? Now that Joe Random is aware that the peanut belongs to the single plant family of Luguminoae, should he gamble against medical advice and chance anaphylactic shock?

Joe Random: Do you smell that? It smells like natural gas. Maybe there is a leak?

Actual Technician: Actually, natural gas has no odour. The smell is added by the utility company. What you are smelling is mercaptan. It is a harmless chemical added to natural gas that contains sulfur which makes it smell like rotten eggs.

Joe Random: Oh, so we are not in danger then?

Actual Technician: Mercaptan is nontoxic, however if we're smelling it, then there is an obvious issue, possibly a gas leak.

Well thank you Bill Nye the Science Guy. That was a long explanation to confirm that there is a potential gas leak. Whether we know the odour was added or not, we know to associate the smell with danger. That is the point of adding that chemical compound. This odd exchange does not help the situation; it only leaves you exposed to a gas leak longer while trying to figure out what is going on.

The Classic One Upper

The Classic One Upper is someone who tries to weigh in on your conversation by adding their own experiences. They will listen to your story and come up with their own version of a similar event. This often has the effect of minimizing your experience or making their own personal encounters more grandiose.

Me: I hit a homerun yesterday. It's my third this year.

Classic One Upper: I once hit three homeruns in one single game.

The Classic One Upper may even catastrophize in order to compete with your encounters.

Me: I dove for a ball today and I broke my arm. I won't be able to finish the season because I will have a cast on for the next 6-8 weeks.

Classic One Upper: That's nothing! Last year I broke my arm in two places. I needed surgery. I ended up with a steel plate in my arm and two screws.

Well then, I guess he won that exchange. How was I supposed to reply to that statement? I didn't even know we were competing. This comment did not add to the conversation, nor did it make me feel better about my season ending injury. Many people believe they are contributing to the conversation by making similar statements. It's often those same comments however that hinder communication.

Some Classic One Uppers or *Toppers* may be uncomfortable or insecure, so they pathologically fabricate lies, using your stories, and making sure the lavish details of their accounts trump your experience. Other Classic One Uppers will self-disclose to contribute to your stories. It's their harmless attempt to add understanding. This act usually takes away the focus from the target, only to shine a spotlight on themselves. I call these people conversation hijackers.

Self-disclosure could be used when attempting to relate to the individual and demonstrate empathy while keeping the focus on the other person. The most important aspect is to turn the conversation back to the target. Like a tennis match among friends, you want to return the ball. That's the area of difficulty for many people. If there is no effort to return the energy, the conversation falls apart. It's the equivalent of smashing the tennis ball during every return. Eventually, people won't want to play anymore. Remember, if you're not adding to the conversation, then you're only taking away.

Here is an example of what some hijackers believe empathy to be:

Joe Random: My mother was recently diagnosed with breast cancer. I am scared for her.

Conversation Hijacker: Yeah, my mom had cancer, it spread to her bones.

Congratulations, conversation commandeered. Should this person take any comfort that some other mother had cancer? How does this information help or add to the conversation?

Her's an example of what I believe empathy and self-disclosure should look like:

"I remember when my mother was diagnosed. It was scary; it even spread to her bones. It will be hard on both of you. Please let me know if you need anything."

In the aforementioned example, the person is informed that you have experienced something similar. You can empathize with them and you are offering support. It ends with the conversation being returned. The point of self-disclosing is to put yourself in the shoes of the other person through shared experienced without revealing too much or taking over.

Captain Cliché

Captain Cliché is an individual who will overuse platitudes to the point where they either lose their original meaning or their desired effect. Lacking originality, they will respond with a trite expression in an attempt to avoid having to use their own thoughts and feelings to answer questions.

I myself do enjoy using clichés, and like to keep a loaded pun when shooting the shit with friends. I understand however, that many examples are outdated or overused to the point where their sharp points have been worn down to a dull stump. Nevertheless, I get annoyed when people hide behind them and use them mechanically in conversations.

I used to have regular conversations with a Captain Cliché. Here's an example of a discussion I had with him regarding some financial struggles he was dealing with.

CC: Well, you know how it is. I am stuck between a rock and a hard place. I've got one foot in the fire, and the other is in the frying pan.

Me: Did you call the bank?

CC: They are all talk, no action.

Me: What are you going to do?

CC: I am damned if I do, and damned if I don't. I am back to the old salt mines

Me: Huh? You back at work?

CC: Another day, another dollar

Me: No layoffs this season?

CC: So far, so good. But it's always the calm before the storm.

Me: Uh....

CC: It is what it is. Everything happens for a reason

Is it? Is it what it is? I despise this saying. Of course it is Captain Obvious. It is such a proclamation of defeat. Is it not just a clever way of saying "fuck it!" Or "What are you gonna do?"

Txtpert In Communication

I like to consider myself to be an old school guy. I don't have a Facebook account and I am not part of the Twitterverse. While I don't like to complicate my life with senseless technology, I am not naïve enough to believe they don't have their use in the modern world. I understand that both in social settings or work settings, people chose to communicate electronically. It can be quicker and easier, or at least it's supposed to be. That's the point. Instant communication at our fingertips.

My issue with these methods of communication is its sheer limitation. I find them ineffective when discussing important or serious matters. Communication via text message and email can be misleading as it lacks expression and tone. I'm sure we've all misinterpreted a message or have been a victim of an auto-correct message that didn't quite make sense.

People who tend to rely on technology to communicate can become passive, avoiding difficult discussions or become aggressive, saying things they normally would never have the courage to say face to face. I have seen people so upset, that they lash out by painting the Facebook walls with derogatory comments, bullying and threatening others from a safe distance. When pressing buttons becomes easier then speaking to one another, we're all at risk of getting lost in the moment. Sometimes, we get impatient with the lag between responses and react by sending a slew of messages until we get a response. This form of communication breeds a generation of less tolerable, bold, passive aggressive people.

I have witnessed countless individuals appearing in court for uttering threats on-line or through text. It has become such a problem with today's youth that we have defined it as cyber bullying[3].

The individuals I see in court have often lashed out during a heated argument escalating to the point where someone said something they could not take back; a comment or threat posted for the world to see. Other individuals chose to utter threats using technology as their vehicle because they lacked the testicular fortitude to do so in person. Computers and smart phones have further perpetuated cowards.

It is not just the text breakups, gossip or threats that annoy me. Modern technology is intended to help us move forward however, instead of it, we have taken steps backwards. We no longer know how to talk to each other. I believe we need to master communicating face to face before we evolve to using technology to assist us.

I was talking with a friend who had been trying her luck with online dating. I was fascinated to discover how small the internet dating world was. She mentioned the name of a guy she had been talking to. It turned out I grew up with this guy. He was a little younger, but we attended the same school and played ball together. So, naturally I didn't cock block him. I talked the guy up. He was a nice guy from a great family. I truly believed they shared common interests. She explained they had been talking for the past week through text but they had not met yet. I thought it was odd to invest that much time without having met this guy. On the other hand, I could appreciate how difficult it is to coordinate schedules. Finally, she explained that they had set up a day to meet. She was considering the traditional diner and a movie date and asked what I thought of her tentative plans. I told her I would start with a drink.

---

3   Cyber bullying is defined as "a young person tormenting, threatening, harassing or embarrassing another young person using the internet or other technologies like cellphones" (Ozier, n.d.).

This way, if the sparks didn't fly I could bail after draining my beer. I wouldn't be committed to the entire evening. She assured me that they had been messaging all week and she had a good feeling about this guy.

Shortly after her date, she informed my wife and I that she was grateful she had altered her plans to a coffee date. She mentioned how painful it was making conversation and how many long awkward silences were shared over the course of a large coffee. She explained that she found it frustrating that two people could carry a text conversation back and forth all day long for seven days but were unable to fill seven minutes of face to face conversation. Needless to say, this date did not inspire another rendezvous.

I was thinking about that situation the other day while waiting in line for my coffee. There were 8 people around me, drones with their faces buried in their phones. Like zombies, everybody took small steps towards the counter, moving in unison, occasionally peeking from their mind control devices for a split second. I heard a phone ring. It belonged to the teenage boy standing in front of me. He appeared so confused. At first, I had assumed he did not recognize the number but then I thought, maybe he did not recognize the feature. I watched him ignore the call, and immediately send a message. He was interrupted mid-message by yet another phone call, which he ignored. I told him "hey Buddy, that instant message, Google machine you have in your hands....also takes phone calls." He answered back saying "Yeah, it's my mom, but I don't have time to talk to her." He ignored the third call and finished sending his message. After that, we stood in silence for over 5 minutes waiting for coffee. Busy Day! He must be too exhausted to take a phone call.

I am willing to bet that the conversation he would have had with his mother would have been less than five minutes. But of course I have no idea of really knowing that. It was just an educated guess as most people avoid the phone as much as possible. There was a situation where my wife and I were having a text conversation about a simple topic and it ended up convoluted and loss in cyberspace. I can assign blame to many contributing factors. My home is a black hole that is not conducive to cell reception. Also, while multitasking, our attention was focused on too many things. This event is now, and will forever be known as the *Cheeseburger incident:*

MJ: What do you want for supper?

Me: I don't care...

Me: Whatever, I am just finishing work and I am leaving soon.

MJ: I don't feel like cooking.

Me: Very well... let me know if you want me to pick something up on my home.

Me: *On my way home.

MJ: What are you in the mood for?

Me: If we order from the pub, I can pick it up.

MJ: We could have pizza?

Me: Ok, but I'll have to detour for that. They don't have that at the pub.

MJ: or we can order burgers...

Me: Sure, but no tomatoes.

MJ: On the pizza?

Me: The burgers!

Me: You just said – or we can order burgers...

MJ: I'll have a wrap.

Me: What!? I thought you wanted burgers.

MJ: If we are ordering from the pub, then I will have a wrap and you can have a burger.

MJ: We can split them half and half.

Me: Ok, I'll have a hamburger.

MJ: I will have the buffalo chicken wrap.

Me: With cheese.

MJ: On the wrap?

Me: No, on my burger.

MJ: I thought you wanted a hamburger not a cheeseburger.

Me: lol, cheeseburger or hamburger with cheese.

MJ: Let's get a fry.

Me: What size? Large?

MJ: For the pizza?

Me: What?

That's when I ended the cheeseburger clusterfuck and used my phone to make an actual call. I am blessed with a wife who has a good sense of humour, so we can laugh it off. Whenever we experience a breakdown in a text communication all I could hear is John Bellushi's character from Saturday Night Live 'Pete from Olympia café' yelling "Cheezborger, cheezborger, cheezborger....no coke, pepsi."

Of course this was a text dialogue that was not riddled with typos and autocorrect insanity. One time she sent me this message:

MJ: There is Foup is the fridge (type o for there is Soup in the fridge)

MJ: It's food. (Auto correct for good)

Only she never corrected her message. She just pressed send and moved on, unaware that I was trying to figure out what this foup was? If you google foup as I have, it comes up as an acronym for Front Opening Unified Pod. This definition did not help me at all.

Another conversation that was funny went like this:

MJ: HOW WAS YOUR DAY?

Me: it's going well. ...WHY ARE WE YELLING

MJ: Sorry. Lol

LOL. I am guilty of misusing this chat jargon. I don't know why we use 'laugh out loud' as regularly as we do? How many of us are truly laughing out loud? I have been caught laughing out loud while looking at my phone in public but it is not a regular occurrence. I just looked at the judging bystanders and pointed to the phone while saying LOL. It does not happen very often. Most 'lol' are grins and smirks but the full blown maniacal laughs are few and far between. Regular hysterical laughter is not funny, it just looks mad. I think lol is probably the most overused cyber shorthand. It's used out of context and often as punctuation or as a filler when people don't know what else to say.

It bothers me that electronic communication allows us the opportunity to edit ourselves. Especially when dealing with conflict. I think it provides us with a false sense of comfort that instills a certain confidence we may lack when interacting with others. It's not real, in the sense that it does not show how we truly behave, how fast we can think on our feet or how witty we actually are. Dropping our shields by putting down the phones, tablets and keyboards forces us to be vulnerable and try to respond assertively.

RULE 2 – KNOW YOUR AUDIENCE

"Half the world is composed of people who have something to say and can't, and the other half who have nothing to say and keep on saying it."
— **Robert Frost**

The starting point to being a great communicator is recognizing who the audience is and how to approach them on an appropriate level.

The second rule "Know Your Audience" is a very important and necessary rule, especially for me. By now, after reading some of my comments and examples you may have come to the conclusion that I can be a bit of an ass sometimes.

No use skirting around the issue anymore. Truth is I have been known to dabble in *Dickery* or *dick-like* behaviour from time to time. How else could I write about this subject? It takes one to know one. We came up with this rule as a loophole to being a dick.

Rule number two is defined as: *If you absolutely, positively must be a dick, then know your audience.*

So why would anyone need to act like a dick?

I think it happens for a number of reasons. People often act without thinking. This can lead to getting caught in a predicament if they did not consider the audience's reaction.

Filter Free

Operating without an internal filter is always a gamble. It's like jumping out of a plane and pulling the cord, wondering if a parachute will emerge or if it's just an empty backpack. Work can be a difficult environment for someone with a loose tongue. Eight-hour days spent in close quarters with people you did not choose to hang out with, knowing full well that some comments could get you in some hot water.

Respecting my workplace filter is one of my biggest challenges. I spend the bulk of my time in court or with clients. I suppress the urge to speak my mind and share my opinions. It's not an easy task for me to do, but I have to force some level of professionalism no matter what I am experiencing in my personal life. Between appointments, I often take the time to debrief and unwind with colleagues, but that normally happens within earshot of management, so I have to keep my professional hat on.

For me, that's where I struggle and often don't refrain from speaking my mind. I am sure my co-workers and supervisor would describe me as filter free. I don't always think to check my surroundings when I go on one of my rants. If only they knew about the things that don't escape my mouth. I am forever doing a balancing act between honest and inappropriate. I view being filterless as delivering an honest message, but without tact.

The problem with being someone who has a faulty filter is that you can be viewed as a clown, and not taken seriously even when in earnest. The filter free population can become reluctant sources of amusement for others. Since people without filters never hold back, others can have a hard time to differentiate when they are joking and when they are being serious. Their intention can be minimized or diminished for this reason. Their messages can be misunderstood, which can lead to hurt feelings. Filter deficient individuals have a tendency to speak before thinking. Sometimes it's hard to hear what they are saying because they are feasting on their foot.

Since filters are an issue at work, I have suggested *Filter Free Fridays⁴*. It's a running joke at work between certain staff; an unwritten rule or understanding that colleagues can be more flexible with their language and let their guard down.

Party Foul

A few years ago I attended a get-together after work. It was a small gathering; I knew most of the people in attendance. There were a few people however, I had not previously met. During this gathering, the kids assembled downstairs while the adults congregated in the kitchen and living room.

While the kids were enjoying YouTube videos, the grownups were ...having drinks and telling jokes. One kid kept coming upstairs to tattle on all the other kids. His mannerisms were priceless. Everyone was laughing at his behaviours; he was extremely agitated and animated, avoiding eye contact while speaking and appeared very awkward. He seemed emotionally stunted and responded in an almost robotic tone; he was systematic. He mentioned during one of his many trips upstairs that someone decided to sit where he had been sitting. "Easy Sheldon Cooper" was my comment. The child's mother gave me the death stare, then advised me her child was diagnosed with Aspergers. I didn't know he was on the Autism Spectrum, but I quickly began to back paddle. I felt like a real dick. I immediately apologized to her and we began discussing the challenges of raising a child with exceptionalities in a small community. Eventually the conversation fizzled out and we focused our conversation on a comedy special featuring Seth Rogan.

Automatically, we began quoting lines from the movie 40-Year-Old Virgin. Specifically the scene where Cal (Seth Rogan) and Dave (Paul Rudd) are playing Mortal Kombat while bantering back and forth on the subject of Dave's celibacy, which quickly turned into an inquiry of Dave's sexual preference.

Cal: ... how do you know I'm gay?

Dave: Because you macramé yourself a pair of jean shorts.

---

4   Please note that *FFF* is neither recognized by management nor endorsed by the union. It does not appear in the policies and procedures or the collective agreement.

Cal: You know how I know you're gay?!

Dave: How?

Cal: I saw you make a spinach dip in a loaf of sourdough bread once.

Dave: You know how I know you're gay?

Cal: How?

Dave: You have a rainbow bumper sticker on your car that says I love it when balls are on my face.

This went on for a while with different degrees of harshness. It evolved to a bit by Bill Burr where his punch line is "Are you some kind of a fag?" The rest of the night seemed to be filled with drinks, snacks and laughter. I had my fill and was ready to call it a night. The host walked me to my car. He informed me that a mutual friend of ours shared some news with him today. It was explained to me that his friend's son informed his family that he was gay.

I asked him why he didn't give me a head's up or at least wind me down while we were pulling out jokes. He just smirked at me and said "What would be the fun in that?" I should have known something was up because he didn't partake in the movie quotes or pile on. He just grinned like he was doing right then.

I never spoke about it to our friends. I know they are good people and supportive parents. I want to believe they were accepting of their child's news but at the same time, I know they didn't need to hear insensitive comments from me. Especially not on the first day their son came out. Despite my insensitive behaviour, I am not someone who makes fun of people's sexual orientation. I make fun of anyone and everyone. That day, I did not respect rule number two. Since I did not know everyone in the room, I should have erred on the side of caution.

Joker

Laughter has been known to be the best medicine and is a great stress reliever. People enjoy making others laugh. This is why we are constantly trying to remember and re-tell jokes to one another. I consider myself to have a healthy sense of humour and I don't hesitate to share my wit with people. Humour plays a big role in my life.

The problem I have is with people who think they are funny. The ones who get caught saying something idiotic or inappropriate and covers it up by saying "just kidding". You know, the type of person who says something out loud, pushes the limits, but as soon as the intended audience does not respond to their liking they say "I was joking." It's as if they were testing the waters but as soon as they realized they've gone too deep they use "humour" as their life vest. It's the equivalent of using "withdrawn."

I can appreciate someone who won't hide behind the false pretense of their humour. Insult comedy is very popular and consists mainly of offensive put downs directed at the target audience. The insult artist. That was my high school experience. My friends and I would meet between classes or during lunch and just ripped into one another.

In my opinion, Don Rickles is the king of insult comedy. He has made a career out of making fun of people. To watch him was astounding. He had a very natural way of interrupting people in order to deliver a quick jab at their expense. Many comedians have tried this approach but few have been able to do it like him. He has been insulting, tormenting and cracking people up for over 50 years.

Growing up in the 80's and 90's, one of my first experiences with rude comedians was watching Andrew Dice Clay. Dressed in his studded leather jacket and shades, this guy looked and acted like a rock star. The Dice Man, with his ever present cigarette. Walking with a swagger he became a rock and roll icon of insults. Arenas and stadiums would be packed with fans. Some were even lucky enough to sit close to the stage, only to be subjected to his harsh brand of humour.

Canadians are seldom thought as rude or crude however my generation remembers Ed the Sock as a legendary pop icon. I grew up watching the cigar smoking, green haired, woolly sock puppet in the 90's. His popularity was largely restricted to Much Music Television (Canada's version of MTV). He became famous for the way he mocked and ridiculed music videos. I always looked forward to his annual 'Fromage' segment. This special aired at the end of the calendar year.

It featured Ed's commentary during the viewing of the cheesiest music videos of that year. His comments and demeanor were typically degrading, overly sexualized and insulting. Ed the Sock may have been a fad, but he grew to celebrity status moving from a television segment to earning his very own show.

I enjoyed watching insult comedy. I still do, but I take exception when it manifests itself in my social life. We pay decent money, or tune in to see the likes of Lisa Lampanelli or Jeff Ross but I am not looking to have their running commentary style in my daily life. There are only a small amount of successful long term insult comics who can pull off this genre of comedy. I find it interesting when Joe Random attempts to use this type of humour in social situations. Not knowing your audience when attempting this risky type of humour can lead to results ranging from mild irritation to feeling like a victim of bullying.

Another dangerous style of humour to adopt socially is shock value humour. This style of humour is intended to stun the audience by pushing the boundaries. Even though this style can be seen as low brow humour, I can still appreciate it at times. Nowadays however, shock humour goes above and beyond toilet humour or dark comedy. Some people will actually make distasteful comments regarding someone's illness or death. They'll make funny references regarding recent tragic events. I have always enjoyed the comedy styles of Norm MacDonald and I appreciate his morbid sense of humour, but his style pales in comparison to Anthony Jeselnik's delivery. Perhaps it's funny to me, because it is on television and I view it as entertainment. I caution anyone who thinks they can pull this off without knowing who their spectators are or without paying attention to the individuals who are within earshot. You can never be certain of people's experiences and values; so playing this risqué comedy card is a gamble.

Here is an example of someone who was attempting to use shock value in a room with individuals he had never met.

Failed Reception

My wife and I were attending an out of town wedding. We travelled several hours to attend the event. I, myself, didn't know many of the guests in attendance.

We were eight to a table and I was fortunate enough to be seated with two couples I had met previously. The two women were my wife's university friends and their respective partners. I got along with one of the guys; we had a lot in common. We had decent conversations with good flow; nothing felt forced. The other individual, I'll call Steve. I had only met Steve twice before. His interests were the complete opposite of mine. Our discussions were laboured and awkward at times. We were having supper the previous night, and he had attempted to make small talk by telling me how expensive his jeans were. He followed that conversational gem by asking me what brand name I was wearing. I am not sure that's a question one man should ever ask another man (Strike one!). That same night, he failed to recognize the Beetles and the Stones on the radio (Strike two!!).

Back to the wedding. We had just enjoyed a short outdoor ceremony, cocktails and a delicious meal. Dessert was being served, the speeches were done; our table was pouring drinks, sharing stories and telling jokes. After every joke, someone came up with a funnier joke. It was now up to Steve. He had been silent for long enough and decided he would start telling jokes. His girlfriend had this mortified look in her eyes as she was pulling on his sleeve. Her eyes, pleading with him to remain quiet. Everyone at the table was anxious to hear this monstrosity of jokes. At this point, I had assumed his girlfriend was involve in the punch line and his anecdote would embarrass her, so of course I was all ears.

Steve smiled and began telling us dead baby jokes. One after another, he was delivering each one with rapid fire succession. He was on his third "zinger" when he realized no one cared for his jokes. I am not comfortable sharing his jokes so I won't repeat them. This type of humour is beyond my understanding. Sitting to Steve's right was a young woman who had recently experienced a miscarriage a few weeks prior to the wedding.

Clearly this man was unaware of this woman's circumstance. I am confident enough to say that had Steve known about her situation, he would not have been so careless with his comments. That is the whole idea behind knowing your audience. When you truly don't know who you are speaking with, sometimes it is better to be cautious.

Chronic Complainer

The Chronic Complainer reminds me of the Classic One Upper, however this individual dwells solely in negativity. The Classic One Downer seems more appropriate. It's easy to mistaken them as a cynic who views their life in a negative way. In reality, these individuals are more complex. Even when things are going their way, the complainer will lament about other aspects of their life.

According to Psychology Today:

The optimists see: a glass half full

The pessimists see: a glass half empty

The Chronic Complainer sees:

"A glass that is slightly chipped, holding water that isn't cold enough, probably because its tap water, when I asked for bottle water and wait, there's a smudge on the rim too; which means the glass wasn't clean properly and now I'll end up with some kind of virus. Why do these things happen to me!?" (Winch, 2011).

The *Chronic Complainer* catastrophizes situations and overuses generalized statements.

- This <u>always</u> happens to me
- I <u>never</u> get a break
- <u>No one</u> cares, <u>everyone</u> is against me
- <u>Every time</u>…

I used to work for a guy who would refer to these individuals as the "needy" people. They are at their best when they appear more miserable than those around them. It is extremely difficult to interact with them.

We all complain, it's only natural to express our dissatisfaction with unmet expectations. However, when complaining becomes our default setting, that is when you know you have become a Chronic Complainer.

Often referred as the pioneer of positive psychology, Martin Seligman has written 20 books and has over 200 publications exploring the advantages to seeing things in a positive way. His work demonstrates that individuals with a positive view on life tend to live longer, have healthier lives, and improve their social life as well as become more productive successful individuals at work. He also cites studies that find that those who refrain from expressing negative emotions and in turn use different strategies to cope with the stresses of life also tend to be happier (Seligman, 2002).

A Chronic Complainer will focus on the elements that make things seem negative. They will only mention their problems and not draw attention to the positive elements in their life. Habitual complainers in your social circle can weigh on others and contribute to people feeling dejected. Chronic Complainers often become ill, sick or suffering from ailments. The toxic behaviour of a Chronic Complainer makes it undesirable for others to be around them. So fixated on their forlorn state, the complainer seldom consider others. I don't think it's a matter of selfishness, rather just lack of awareness. I am not certain they know how they actually come off.

Awakening

There is someone currently in my life that resembles the Chronic Complainer. I won't go into great detail as to who this person is for fear it may cause me grief or subject me to complaints. Let's just say I am close to someone who begins conversations on a negative note. Many of our telephone conversations begin with "Do you know who just died?" What a way to start a conversation. Nine out of ten times I have no idea who the departed was. My grandfather's third cousin? The person I last saw when I was 8 months old at a family reunion?

That may have been a slight exaggeration but I digress. This individual once broke his foot, which required surgery. That, in itself is a reason to complain, so I think a reasonable amount of slack was awarded. I was attending a wake with this individual. I am not certain who had passed but I was going to pay my respects to the family. The deceased was an elderly gentleman who had been ill for some time, and although tragic, was not a sudden death. It was still sad, but no one was surprised by his passing.

As we prepared to meet the family in the procession line, the widow asked how we were. I believe this is one of those empty questions grievers ask in an attempt to normalize difficult situations. Most people just nod, offer their sympathy and move on up the line. I had the misfortune of being behind the Chronic Complainer.

The widow thanked us for attending and automatically asked how we were. I don't think she realized the can of worms she had opened. I stood in line between the corpse and the widow, listening to the *Chronic Complainer* explain every ache and pain pre and post-surgery. Suddenly I was envious of the stiff to my right resting peacefully, lucky to not have to sit through re-runs of the "sad and painful." The situation ended with widow comforting the Chronic Complainer at her husband's wake. I honestly had to walk away.

Events such as these happen regularly in our ever day life. Recently, I was at my local veterinary clinic picking up medication for my dog. I was waiting in line to be served when I spotted a woman and her crying child sitting behind me. They were in the process of putting their dog down. Ahead of me was an irate man disputing his bill. He was dumfounded that it came up to $290. The man appeared outraged. He turned towards us and exclaimed, "He ain't even sick! Can you believe this? All that money for a healthy dog." I would like to believe this man was ignorant of Fido's fate and how sad that family was. Judging by the mother's reaction, I think she was ready to shell out a small fortune in order to save her dog.

First World Problems

I always found this term to be interesting and was curious as to its origin. I looked it up and discovered a model that groups countries in three separate tiers (First, Second, and Third World, 2021).

The first consists of countries of common interest that were allied during and after the Second World War. These countries have similar capitalist ideas and are seen as industrious and wealthy. These are countries from North America, Europe, East Asia and Australia.

The second tier represents the debunked communist social countries formerly known as the Eastern Block and the Soviet Union. Also included are China as well as some of the Turk states.

The third tier comprises of neutral countries not aligned with either tier as well as the developing countries of Africa, Asia and Latin America.

The term First World Problem was accepted by the Oxford dictionary in 2012 and is defined as: "a relatively trivial or minor problem or frustration implying a contrast with serious problems such as those that may be experienced in developing world" (Oxford Languages, 2021).

As I understand it, this term typically refers to annoyances that occur to individuals living in a wealthy industrialized nation. People constantly in distress, announcing the difficulties they're experiencing. In hindsight, these seem like frivolous, minor issues that usually have little effect in our lives and would most likely confuse people from under-developed environments.

It's a common problem that is only an issue in our culture. First World Problems often occur when were unsatisfied with the amount or quality of inconsequential possessions. We exert a great deal of energy acquiring material belongings, especially electronics. Listen to your friends and colleagues first world problems and you'll probably discover how often it revolves around gadgets, trinkets and smart phones.

- "There's no free Wi-Fi at this hotel."
- "I only have one bar of service in this suite"
- "How can I update my Facebook status if I don't have service?"
- "The storm has knocked down the satellite signal again."

Ok, that last one was definitely me. I lose my mind when the service gets knocked out while I am watching hockey, but I understand that these are very insignificant issues when we consider war, famine, illness and homelessness. I am reminded of Weird Al Yankovic's song

"First World Problems" off his 'Mandatory Fun' album. The song starts like this:

"My maid is cleaning my bathroom so I can't take a shower. When I do the water starts getting cold after an hour. I couldn't order off the breakfast menu 'cause I slept in till two."

I've only heard the song a handful of times, but I thought the lyrics were pretty clever. Some lines I enjoyed in this tune include

"Tried to fast forward the commercials, can't I'm watching live TV." And "My house is so big, I can't get WI-FI in the kitchen."

This American parodist has gained popularity with his satiric humour. Once again, he works his particular brand of magic, making light of popular culture in addressing this theme. You don't have to be a fan of the Polka Pop artist to appreciate his message. I think, as we continue to spoil ourselves with new smart phones and quicker bandwidth, we're potentially creating a generation of First World Problem complainers.

I certainly understand the global concept and have been guilty of such lamentations. When I lose my television feed or when my cell service craps out, I am the first person to gripe. I don't have to empathize with under-developed cultures to realize that this type of grumbling only leads to me being a dick.

"I have uptown problems...but you're not a problem at all." This great quote was plucked from the movie "Money Ball." Brad Pitt's character Billy Bean, who is the General Manager of the Oakland Athletics, says that line to his daughter when discussing the subject of losing his job. Uptown problems, which is to say it is not really a problem at all. It's difficult to complain about these things when you consider the money these athletes get paid to entertain us. That's how I feel when I am bellyaching about poor cell service to someone who can't afford a phone.

In my personal experience I don't have to go across the ocean to see how making First World Problems statement makes me sound insensitive. There are plenty of people among the first tier who are impoverished, go to sleep hungry or are dealing with health issues.

From a local perspective, there are many under privileged individuals in our own back yards.

First World Folly

I was attending a case conference with multiple community partners. The purpose of this meeting was to make sure all the agencies were on the same page. We would discuss everyone's role in order to maximize our efforts and to ensure there were no gaps or duplications of services. We were sitting around, sipping coffee, and waiting for the client to arrive so we could begin.

Due to a recent fire, this individual had lost everything. He was homeless, surviving by accessing food banks, soup kitchens and couch surfing. Since he was homeless, he had become somewhat transient and did not have a phone to use in order to follow-up with us. I had lost contact with him temporarily, but had high hopes he would attend today's meeting.

He arrived almost 30 minutes late. He walked in and apologized stating that he had missed the bus, but had no way of contacting us to advise us of his delay because he had no phone. One of the community partner was shaking her head. She had a sympathetic look in her eyes and blurted out:

"I understand. I had a rough weekend myself. I was at the cottage, but I left my phone charger at home. I was without a phone for like 18 hours."

She stopped talking at that point, probably because she felt several pair of eyes staring at her. She must have realized how ridiculous she sounded to him because for the remainder of the meeting she kept her head down and spoke minimally.

I Told You So

Is there a more condescending statement in the English language? (That was an Askhole Rhetorical question). Saying 'I told you so' is a way to highlight other people's flaws and remind them that you were right. It's implying that they ignored your warning and now it's time for you to gloat about their misfortune.

It's as if the price of ignoring your advice is to kick them while they're down. It's a bold, direct statement that instils shame and blame. Frankly, I'd rather be hit in the nuts by a whiffle ball bat. Making such statement is counter-productive to the flow of any conversation. It's just an immature act to let the other person know that their way of thinking is inferior to yours.

What I find aggravating is when people add the disclaimer "hate to say it..." right before dropping the "I told you so" bomb. Let's face it, if you're the type of person who doesn't hesitate to cash in on "I told you so" moments, you definitely don't hate bringing it up, so you can omit the disclaimer. Does it somehow justify the behaviour? "I totally hate to be a dick in this situation, however, I will consciously chose to act like one anyways".

Everyone enjoys being right. There is a powerful, satisfying feeling that comes with this. Some people feel this way when they think they are right, regardless of the outcome. The need for affirmation is so overwhelming for some people that they will use this saying freely without considering how their statement impacts others.

Don Cherry

Donald Stewart Cherry is a National Hockey League icon. The retired player and coach is mostly renown for being a sports commentator. He's recognized as a very outspoken and opinionated analyst. The snappy dresser doesn't hide his beliefs or points of view. When he's passionate about certain topics, he's been scrutinized for being politically incorrect on air. He's been criticized more than once for bringing up controversial topics.

His love for Canada and our culture has been so extreme that some people view him as being culturally insensitive towards other nations. It's love or hate with Don Cherry. Most people I know find themselves at one end or the other of the spectrum. I seldom meet people who fall in the middle. I, myself, love him. I really enjoyed watching his television segment and I used to believe it was the highlight of Hockey Night in Canada. I am wise enough now to be entertained by "Coach's Corner" but I don't have to accept everything that is said as gospel.

My issue with this Canadian treasure is the amount of absolute statements he makes on a weekly basis. He often punctuates his statements with "mark my words" or "you heard it here first." God forbid he strikes oil with one of his comments because he will replay his previously recorded statement on air during his segment, just to provide proof of his prediction. The ultimate "I told you so." This typically took place while co-host Ron MacLean sat to his right holding a painfully awkward grin. Just once, I would have liked for Ron to go on a Don Cherry-like rant.

"Why don't we play all the times you were wrong instead of making the video crew sift through all this footage. It is like a scavenger hunt, trying to find that needle in the haystack clip of when you told the world you were right and it was true. God knows there's not enough time to highlight every time you were wrong with a 7 minute segment, Kingston Boy!"

All kidding aside, no one wants to be around someone who is constantly telling you that you are wrong and they are right. I don't know if Don Cherry's television persona seeps into his personal life, but there's a reason his on air time was limited. Since the original publishing of this book, Mr. Cherry's services are no longer rendered on air due to his flagrant violations of rule 1 and 2.

Socially, if you are the type of person who makes it a point to advertise your successful predictions, you risk pushing people away, especially if it's highlighting someone's failure. No one will want to be around you. Unfortunately, when that happens and you find yourself alone, there will be no one there to say, "I told you so."

25 Cent Bet

My brother, Jodie and I have strong personalities. I could say the same thing about my sister, but she is several years younger and we didn't grow up arguing half as much as my brother and I did.

My brother and I are less than two years apart in age. We shared a bedroom for the first 12 years of my life. He was my first friend and has since become my best friend. Growing up however, there were many incidences where he was a thorn in my paw.

Jodie is the oldest and was always more academically gifted. For this reason, I often assumed he was right and many disagreements went unchallenged. Jodie is a very intelligent person but he could stoop down to my level in no time. He was the kind of kid growing up that re-invented or modified the rules mid-game to his benefit. Although he was considered an introverted child, he could be very outspoken and opinionated, especially when facing an "I told you so" moment. As we grew older and matured a little, the disagreements diminished and so did the resentment.

I believe the reason the disagreements are now fewer is because we came up with the perfect solution. Although he may take full credit for it, the truth is I don't remember how it all started. What I do know is that it works and it has forever changed our relationship.

This example may not be the first time we used it, but it's one of my earliest recollections of the bet. I remember talking about bad hockey trades and acquisitions.

Jodie: ...Daniel Briere – that was a bad signing for the Flyers.

Me: It was a huge contract, considering he has not exceeded last year's performance.

Jodie: Exceed? He was terrible this year!

Me: I didn't think he was terrible. It's hard to thrive in that environment.

Jodie: His numbers were at an all-time low.

Me: Not his scoring. I think he did as well as he had done in the past.

Jodie: No way!

Me: Yes...way!

Jodie: Vingt-Cinq cents? (French equivalent for a quarter).

Me: On what? (I had to be specific. If I didn't nail the language he would find a way to weasel his way out).

Jodie: His goals. They have to be comparable to last year.

Me: Give or take one...or two.

When faced with a disagreement where facts are missing, we apply the twenty five cent rule. It only applies in situations where you can prove the other person wrong. Once the bet is made, it's up to the person who was challenged to come up with the supporting evidence.

The disagreement is over once the bet has been acknowledged by both parties. In previous years, a simple conversation like this would have snowballed to something ridiculous. Instead, the bet is in effect and the conversation (regarding this specific topic) can only resume when the facts are checked. You can't add information or defend your position. Sometimes curiosity gets the worst of my brother and he'll do the leg work. In these modern times, powered by Google, most of us have the answers at the touch of our fingertips.

Jodie: Hey Plute (that's what he calls me).

Me: Hey!

Jodie: I owe you a quarter.

Me: Oh!?

Jodie: Briere. He scored 32 goals with the Sabres last year. This year he finished the season with 31 goals as a Flyer.

Me: It was that close?

Jodie: Yeah, but he had 22 less assists and his +/- was at an all-time low with -22

Although he did admit that he owed me the quarter, he also attempted to justify his position with his "yeah, but" statement[5]. Ultimately, it was his way of saying I was right while saying "I told you so." As I mentioned before, he likes to modify the rules to his benefit.

The monetary value is also an important factor because the bet has to be worth something. There has to be something tangible to win or lose. Something worth arguing over, but not so much that you need to re-mortgage your home. The value can't be so grand that it could be used to bully the other to stand down or submit their position. The new piece of currency in our social circle is the Filet-O-Fish (I'm NOT loving it). Essentially, the loser of the bet must consume this sandwich while the victor watches in amusement.

---

5   "yeah but ..." remember that in the middle of every butt is an asshole.

The fact is, the knowledge of Daniel Brier's stats for the 2007-2008 season is not worth much to me, but I'll wager a quarter if it proves my brother wrong. An empty wager is meaningless. I remember playing Texas Hold 'em at a fundraiser (for no money).

Dealer: Everyone gets $100 worth of chips.

Me: What is the chip value?

Dealer: White ones are $5...

Me: The blue one?

Dealer: $10

Me: ...the black ones, the red ones?

Dealer: ...$50...$100

Me: Nice, what's the buy in?

Dealer: These chips can't be redeemed

Me: Huh?

Dealer: There is no real value to any of these chips. It's just for fun.

Me: Fun? In that case, I am all in. Yay fun!

Imposers

I'm a very opinionated person. I know this; however I seldom force my opinions on others. At least I make a conscious effort to refrain from doing so. When someone says something ignorant I'm usually quick to make comments, however I'm wise enough to understand that forcing my opinions on anyone will lead me nowhere. Most people who have a rigid way of thinking will likely ignore any relevant data presented to them, so opinions will often fall on deaf ears.

My opinion, after all is my point of view regarding my beliefs and values. It is not a fact. I immediately become on edge whenever someone presents their opinions as fact. Too often people cannot distinguish between facts and opinions.

Fact: Roger Clemens was pulled out of the game in the 6th inning.

Opinion: Roger Clemens should have been pulled out of the game earlier because he had nothing left in the tank.

Facts are raw data supporting a comment or an opinion. The above example of the opinion could be supported by facts and evidence to build an argument but it remains an opinion, and not fact. People are not quick to change their opinions without being presented with a set of facts. I often witness people battle, pinning their opinions against each other, but in the absence of any hard facts or data there is no reason one would budge from their initial position.

One of my favorite arguments remains: "The Montreal Canadiens are/is the best hockey team."

Many people would agree with this statement. The Canadiens have one of the biggest fan bases across the world and one of the most successful dynasties. However, this statement is not a fact. It would be a great topic for debate. What's the basis for this statement? Does this absolute, broad statement indicate that this team is statistically better than all the other teams? In every category? Of all time? Does it mean the Montreal Canadiens have had more success, more wins, or more Stanley Cup victories? Nothing about that statement makes it factual. There is no additional information to support the statement.

Fact: The Montreal Canadiens are the team to have won the most Stanley Cups in the history of the NHL.

Fact: Last year the Habs dominated most statistical categories, earning them several team awards and individual achievements.

It's long winded, but it's true. Everyone has an opinion and many people believe theirs is right. I used to work for a guy who would tell me "opinions are like assholes, everyone has them." Another wise person added "opinions are like farts, hard to hold in, and when you let one out people are going to know about, it may offend some and it can also clear a room."

So why do people offer their opinions to others?

- They are insecure and need their opinions validated
- They don't understand or can't accept that there can be more than one answer
- They misunderstood your position
- They love to argue and debate

- They don't know when to let it be, let it go or drop it

Soul Solicitors

Religion is one of those taboo off-limit topics that is often banned from school or workplace environments. The subject is extremely objectionable and reflects personal choice.

I don't consider myself to be an overly religious person but when someone is trying to draw me into a conversation or argument regarding my spiritual beliefs, I typically abstain. I refuse to get sucked into their forceful vortex. It's hard for me to ignore certain statements made in ignorance, but I recognize the value in not engaging. Often, I will ask the other person what the purpose of the conversation is. What is the expectation and what is to be gained? If it's to hear the other person's opinion or their take on that particular topic, then I may entertain them however, if the intent of the discussions is to sway me into changing my belief system then they are wasting their time.

I'm very curious about the difference in religions so I often ask questions because I lack knowledge; I'm ignorant to many aspects of other spiritual or cultural beliefs. Regardless of my opinions, it's not one I feel the urge to discuss or impose on anyone. Some people subscribe to blind faith. There is no strong data supporting their actions or beliefs. It's their faith, so who am I to judge?

Certain people of strong faith feel the need to solicit their religion to others and are constantly attempting to inform, educate, save and for lack of a better word, recruit new members. That's their prerogative. What frustrates me is when I get surprised at my doorstep to discuss religion or my relationship with God (Relationship status: It's complicated). My reply is often the same.

"I have my beliefs and I respect that you have yours. I don't feel like talking about my faith with you."

This answer doesn't always get me in the clear, which can lead me to address the situation with a simple assertive "I" statement.

"I feel frustrated when you ambush me in my home, I would like for you to leave."

When the tenacious individual(s) persist, I'm required to crank up my response and I typically cross over and adopt a passive-aggressive approach.

"Listen, I don't go to your home to confront you or challenge your belief system, please leave."

For some, this is enough and they will nod and walk away. Others however, are bold enough to suggest I'm welcome to attend their home and open a dialogue about their deity. This is where my patience wears thin. These Soul Solicitors are as relentless as telemarketers.

Religion aside, there are many sensitive topics people avoid discussing because it elicits so much passion. I once got sucked into a pro-life, pro-choice debate with two feminists. There was really no way of getting out of that jam without appearing like a dick to one or both debaters (See rule 3) because of their overuse of absolute statements. These bold declarations provided me with little to no room for debate. When we tear down their statements, they were nothing but personal beliefs that vary from person to person based on values, ethics and life experience.

Vegan / Vegetarians

I don't mean to limit this category to only those who deprive themselves of delicious meat. I include all extreme dieters or people who have radical lifestyles which they attempt to impose on you.

Have you ever met a vegan who has not advertised their lifestyle choice to you? I guess that could be a trick question. Withdrawn on the *askhole* question. What I meant to say is I have noticed that many vegans pretentiously go out of their way to advertise their ultimate sacrifice and I was hoping you did too.

So, you don't want to eat meat? No problem, more for this carnivore. I love meat. Red meat and I have never felt bad for its ingestion. Of course, my overall consumption is not as extreme as it once was. I have a wise wife that has exercised the practice of moderation in my life. This recent decrease is more out of concern for my health and less about the helpless animals. Whenever my wife is away, she will prepare a full menu of meals in advance. These meals often include an abundance of vegetables, as she fears I will get scurvy from my poor eating habits.

Fact is (starting a sentence with "fact is" does not make it a fact) I don't trust someone who does not eat meat. That is my opinion and I may share it alone. I am certainly not expecting or looking for anyone to accept it as fact. I am not saying "non-meat eaters" should not be trusted. I am saying that as a rule, I do not. Just joking, withdrawn.

There's something frustrating with being judged by someone because of your eating habits. I had one of my first awkward encounters a few summers ago. I was battling a summer cold and dealing with seasonal allergies. My infinite struggle to breath was a nightmare and responsible for my lack of sleep. It took a Herculean effort to complete the most mundane tasks. One day, I was winded after walking two flights of stairs. I had to take a break and catch my breath but what took the wind out of my sails was the shocking comments that came next.

"You should do CrossFit with me; eliminate red meat from your diet. You'll be in better shape."

I was so thankful that this person was able to judge me based on a small glimpse of my life.

"Thank you for offering solace in the shape of a lifestyle change."

Would I benefit from CrossFit and watching my diet? Absolutely, who wouldn't? I would also benefit from not smoking, avoiding empty calories, carbs and gluten. It's not something I'm ready to commit to. Also, I refuse to believe these extreme changes would cure my cold or my allergies. This situation was resolved with over-the-counter anti-histamines, chugging a bottle of Buckleys and catching up on some much needed sleep.

It's as if the individuals who choose to starve themselves, always attempt to rationalize their decisions. They deprive themselves of delicious treats, work out twice a day, seven days a week and justify their actions by preaching and recruiting others. Sorry, you can keep the purple Kool-Aid. I am not interested. I am Freshie guy[6].

---

6   Freshie is Canadian alternative to Kool-Aid available in the 80's, popular among us in the lower to middle socio-economic bracket.

Knowing your audience is a cardinal rule.

Awhile back I was living in one of our major cities. I was in my early twenties, working full-time in the downtown core of this metropolis. Like any typical Canadian, I preferred to start my morning with a Tim Horton's coffee. This particular morning however, would start differently and would have an everlasting impact on my life. The previous evening I had dropped off my vehicle at a shop located next to a shopping mall. I was advised my car would be ready in the morning and I could pick it up on my way into work.

I walked the ten blocks to the shop but it was not opened yet. I decided to test my patience by venturing into the mall and treating myself to a gourmet caffeinated beverage. Armed with a good book and a pocket full of change I was prepared to wait and get my fix. I went through all the necessary motions (in my head), speaking gibberish in an attempt to order a large coffee using the barista's native tongue: pretentious. When I arrived at the coffee shop I was relieved that it was relatively empty. It was just me in line waiting behind a hipster girl who was wearing several mismatched scarves and vintage buttons. With my guard down, I uttered the phrase "Large coffee, 2 sugars."

Here's a great example of the importance of knowing your audience. When a simple looking guy dressed in ripped jeans and a plaid shirt[7] approaches your counter for a large coffee, don't act like you don't understand what he's saying. I ordered it in both French and English to avoid any language barrier issues.

I'm sure she had no issues with the hipster who had ordered a half-caf, low fat, soy latte warmed at 120 degrees. My angst-filled barista understood that, but could not decipher "large, black coffee with 2 sugars." I was met with an expressionless face. It was disturbing and troublesome. I added "...it means no milk or cream..." We both engaged in an intense stared down that probably lasted twenty seconds but felt like an eternity. Finally, rolling her eyes, she looked back at her supervisor and repeated the order in the form of a question. "Large coffee? Black, two sugars?" The statement was punctuated with a cocked eyebrow and a puzzled look. My blood pressure must have been spiking because

7   Please note, this was the early 2000's, before pre-ripped jeans were sold at designer prices. It was before the hipster and lumbersexual fad.

I felt like Michael Douglas in the movie Falling Down. The supervisor stepped in.

Supervisor: Bold, dark or light roast?"

Me: "Whatever is hot" I replied in an abrasive manner.

Me: "The biggest format you have." I added before hearing about their foreign sizes.

Supervisor: "Sweetener and sugar are at the end of the counter. What is your name?

Now it was my turn to have a dumb look on my face.

Me: "My name?"

Barista: "Yes, your name, so we can call it out when your order it ready."

Call out my order? I was so confused. I just want a coffee? Just pour it and let's go!

Me: "Jay"

Barista: "Dave?"

Me: "Jason"

Barista: "David"

Sure! Whatever, let's just get this show on the road.

Me: "Exactly, only it is spelled and pronounced differently."

I hoped they wouldn't ask for identification when I presented myself to claim my coffee. I looked around the empty room, no one in line, let alone in the entire mall so why the hell do they need to call out my name?

In the amount of time it would take me to grind the beans and percolate a pot of coffee this light-bright was able to pour me one cup. Finally I heard "Dave!" "David?" She was looking right at me, waiting for a response. I was busy daydreaming of all those diners and breakfast joints. I miss those rough looking waitresses who would call you dear or sweetheart while serving you endless coffee. I won't get into how much I paid for this beverage because that's an entirely different source of frustration. She eventually gave up and just handed me my cup. I had time to kill, but I refused to do it in this café. I grabbed 2 packages of raw sugar and headed out into the mall.

I walked to the other end of the shopping complex, sat down and read my book. After a few pages, I removed the lid of my coffee so I could add the sugar. I realized right away that my frustrations were not ending, there were just beginning. I stared at the caramel coloured coffee, the same daft way I stared at my 10th grade math homework; simply perplexed. That's an odd looking black coffee was my first reaction. Those idiots couldn't even get my order right. It was not like it was so busy and they were overwhelmed and my order was not so intricate that it was easy to mess up. This had to have been intentional. I didn't accidently get someone else's order, I was their only customer. Plus, it said Dave on my cup. Dave does not like cream! Of course I said this to no one but myself and proceeded to drink my caffeinated disaster. A quarter of my cup was drained when my gut began doing backflips.

My next adventure took place in one of the worst possible settings: the mall washroom. The only reason for me to attend this part of the building was by absolute necessity. I did the "shitty shuffle" (you know the walk, where you tighten your asshole, straighten your legs and slide your feet instead of lifting them off the ground) for over 200 feet before relief was in sight. As I entered the restroom, I was greeted by what appeared to be a homeless man grooming himself. He said "Hello" in a jovial voice, but I did not reply. I gave him a head nod, acknowledging the stranger's presence while avoiding eye contact. This is a respectful way of greeting anyone at the john while discouraging further conversations. My non-verbal language let him know he was not invisible, but also that we were not going to discuss it.

This has nothing to do with the socio-economic status of the stranger. It was simple bathroom etiquette. I was not bothered by his presence. He was doing his thing and at any moment I would be doing my own thing. I was more concerned with the state of the public restroom toilet seat. I am not a germaphobe, but at the same time I don't welcome the idea of sitting bare ass on a seat where countless people of questionable hygiene have been dropping deuces. I forced myself into believing that since it was so early in the morning the facility would still be clean. I was faced with a situation that required less thinking and more doing. Lucky for me, the coffee did all the work and my instincts kicked in.

I automatically assumed a power squat position, focused on keeping a hover over the petri dish of human bacteria. My focus was rattled when I heard "... gonna be a nice one today." The stranger's voice echoed from outside my stall. Despite the fact that I had remained silent when I strolled past him, walking like the emperor penguin, he was talking to me as if we were in the middle of a conversation. Bathroom etiquette suggests eye contact, and conversation should be avoided at all cost. Also, staring at another man's unit is a faux pas, but that's not applicable in this situation[8].

He had violated these rules, and yet I had not replied. Perhaps he was speaking to himself? He followed up with "Oh yeah... it's going to be a warm one. I hope it is not too muggy." Now it was awkward. I had finished my business, the paperwork was done but it didn't sound like the man had left yet. I couldn't hear him anymore but I sensed that he was still there. Anyone who loiters in the men's room is automatically labelled and judged as creepy. I checked my watch and knew I couldn't wait him out so I decided to bite the bullet and go wash my hands.

This is where the weird got weirder. As I exited the stall, I spotted the man standing in front of the mirror. He was shirtless with a face full of shaving cream. He had chosen the middle sink to remove his whiskers. I can appreciate him wanting to shave and I can even be sold on the idea that he did not want to get his shirt wet or dirty but a violation of the buffer rule was unacceptable. This guy knew I was there. He could have occupied one of the corner sinks to avoid any potential contact, especially given the fact that he was shirtless.

I do not believe this weird, shirtless guy had any sexual intentions. I just didn't want my personal space invaded by a topless dude in a public restroom. To add to the creep factor, this guy was staring at me through the mirror. He tilted his head towards the stall and actually asked me "how was that?" He turned his gaze from the mirror to look at me. He was inches away from my face, but I kept looking straight ahead. I could see his bulbous gin blossom nose with a detailed road map displaying

---

8   For more bathroom rules check out *www.goodmenproject.com*

his struggles and journey on Allison Road[9]. Our eyes eventually met through the mirror's reflection and I gave him the "I'm not impressed" look while washing my hands, a look that George Costanza[10] would have been proud of. An exaggerated eye roll punctuated with a sarcastic grin. Our interaction ended with him slapping me on the back and telling me to "take 'er easy." I just walked away shaking my head.

Appropriately annoyed (at lease in my mind), I arrived at the garage. It was now open and I was ready to reclaim my car. I couldn't wait to jump in my vehicle, battle my way through traffic and put this morning behind me. Instead, I was greeted by a gum-smacking, mouth breathing idiot who looked at me with a vacant stare.

Me: I'm here to pick up my car

Idiot: We just opened

Me: I dropped it off yesterday and was advised to pick it up first thing in the morning.

Idiot: Uh....we just opened?

Uh-Oh! We have a moron! And was that a question? I repeated the instructions, this time in French, only to discover this person was an idiot in both official languages.

I walked past the clerk's counter, through the "employee only" door and flagged the mechanic I had previously dealt with. He explained to me that my car was not ready. They had apparently attempted to contact me on my cell phone (that I never kept charged). My car needed a part and they were out of stock.

Mechanic: Sorry you had to make the trip down here. We tried calling you.

Me: Yeah, my phone's dead. It's ok. I'll just take the subway to work.

Mechanic: It will be ready for you this afternoon. You want a lift to the closest station?

Me: (Checking my watch) Sure that would be helpful.

---

9   Alternative rock reference: Gin Blossoms are an American band from the late 80's with hits such as *Hey Jealousy, I'll Follow You Down, 'Til I Hear it From You* and *Allison Road.*

10 George Louis Costanza was a character from the television show Seinfeld (1989-1998) played by Jason Alexander.

Mechanic: Let me buy you a coffee.

He must have noticed my hesitation and apprehension because he suggested we hit a Tim Horton's in lieu of the hoity toity place in the mall where they make even a simple thing complicated.

I thought, this would surely be the turning point of my difficult day. I had a fresh cup of Joe and a twenty minute subway ride to work. I figured it was better than being grid-locked in traffic. I still had my book and a piping hot black coffee with 2 sugars (no cream). By now, I'm sure you've realized that I hate people. Not specific individuals but people as a collective. If you could imagine how cramped a subway car gets during morning rush-hour, then perhaps you could empathize with my discomfort and annoyance.

I sat down at the far end of the car, buried my face in my book and placed my earbuds in my ear. It's funny how clueless some people can be. Although I appeared to be enjoying music and a book, I was still subjected to people's stupidities. At one of the first stops I spotted a young couple in my peripheral vision. What caught my eye was their clothing. He was wearing an old school Thor T-shirt and she was wearing a vintage cobra tank top. I was truly impressed with their duds. I assume they mistook my interest in their attire as an invitation to sit down next to me because they bee-lined towards me, ignoring vacant seats along their path. Aware of their unwavering gaze, I kept my eyes on my book. Unfortunately, this only lasted for another subway stop.

Guy: What you listening to?

Me: Nothing...

There was a long pause with an awkward silence. He kept looking at me, so I pulled the earbud cord out of my pocket, revealing that it was not plugged to anything.

Me: I just have them in my ears to avoid having to talk to people. Sometimes I'll even bob my head as if I'm keeping the beat.

Guy: That's brilliant.

He exclaimed this while punching the girl playfully on her shoulder.

The guy kept laughing, but the irony was lost on him. I put my head down and continued to read.

Guy: What's your stop?

Me: Sorry...

I shouted while pointing to my earbuds

Guy: What is your stop?

Me: ...I can't hear you.

This time tapping my feet and bobbing my head, I kept my head down until I reached my stop. I understand I was acting like a dick. I was having one hell of a morning and it was not even 8:30 am yet. I had encountered too many rule 2 violators for me to exercise my non-dickery personality. Hence the purpose of the second rule. The better you know your audience the more liberal you can be with your Dickery.

RULE 3 –
NEVER BREAK UP A GIRL FIGHT

"Girls compete with each other,
women empower one another."
— Unknown

Isn't this common sense?

I know it makes perfect sense to me. I also know some of you are giggling with excitement at the prospect of two girls fighting, while others are judging me as a male chauvinist for even mentioning it. I can understand why, after all most men would agree there's something perverse and wicked about two girls duking it out.

I have been asked why men are so enthralled with the idea of seeing two girls fighting. Although I have no conclusive data to support my theory, I will offer the following hypotheses:

1. It's out of character

Girls across the globe are viewed as the fairer sex and kinder gender. We're raised to believe men seek resolution through violence while our counterparts are more practical. They use their words as an alternative to violence to resolve problems. Stumbling on a girl fight is a rarity, like discovering a unicorn.

2. Men are simple

Men are such simple creatures, like pigs. Knowing there tends to be more clutch and grab happening in a girl fight, we are hopeful one or both of the contestants will give us a peep show. In our minds, it's reasonable to assume a blouse could be torn or a tank top strap could be damaged in a fight. If Janet Jackson was able to provide millions of viewers with a nip slip during a song and dance routine, there is a possibility of a wardrobe malfunction to occur amid the chaos.

3. They may kiss

You can thank the creative minds and film makers of the San Fernando Valley for contributing to men's unrealistic sexual expectations when it comes to girl on girl fantasies. These southern California misfits use many integral plot twists in their movies. They depict adrenaline filled women which turn into an aphrodisiac so powerful it transforms a heated battle into a steamy make-out session leading to a classic lesbian scene.

4. The entertainment factor

Men like watching violence. It could be hockey goons dropping their gloves or two MMA fighters squaring off in the octagon. Men will even look for excitement while watching baseball. A sport so mundane it's compared to watching paint dry. Some, however, will tune in for a game or the highlights on the off chance that there is a bench clearing brawl.

Girls have been described as having a rather unorthodox fighting style, quite unlike Rowdy Ronda[11], but let's be honest she's the exception, not the rule. Girl's fighting styles have led men to bully others by saying such demeaning phrases as "you fight like a girl."

Alltogether, we have an unusual and rare event that can lead to partial nudity with the possibility of witnessing an intense sexual encounter; throw in an open bar, some hot wings and a decent soundtrack, and it may be describing Heaven to a lot of men (and women).

---

11 Ronda Jean Rousey is a mixed martial artist who won a bronze medal in judo at the 2008 Olympics. She was also a Strikeforce and UFC Bantamweight champion.

I believe this concept is glorified because when we think of girls fighting, we picture the Divas of wrestling or high maintenance girls in a hair pulling slap fest. Popular culture has capitalized on this stereotypical way of thinking. We've seen mud wrestling, foxy boxing and Jerry Springer. This exaggerated cliché has led to men minimizing and belittling any disagreement among women and labelling it as a 'cat fight.' This, in my opinion indicates that these narrow minded individuals can't envision women having a dispute or a difference of opinion without being "catty." I find that to be a sad thought.

The theme of rule 3 has been mentioned in television sitcoms such as *Seinfeld*, *The Big Bang Theory* and by the ultimate dater Barney Stinson in *How I Met Your Mother* (Kuhn, 2008). However I actually first had the idea while watching the *Californication* series. In the episode entitled "Blues from Laurel Canyon" (Season 2, episode 11), Hank Moody gets flack for separating a girl fight. I was kidding when I initially suggested this rule, but it didn't take a lot of afterthought to make this a serious rule.

I believe men like the idea of a girl fight more than the reality of the event. This spectacle, especially live, creates a rush in men that increases our heart rate and blood pressure. But as soon as someone gets hurts, the fantasy evaporates and the rush dissipates. So why do I think it should be a rule?

Let's remove all elements of fantasy or sexuality from this equation and consider the women in our lives. Think about your sister, mother, your mother-in-law or spouse. Ask yourself about the benefits of getting involved in one of their arguments. From personal experience, I know better than to involve myself in an argument between my wife and her mother.

Here is an example, using a made up scenario. 100% made up (remember that, Ma).

Wife: (After being hung up on by her mother) Can you believe her? What a bitch.

Me: Yeah

Wife: Who? My mom?

Me: I'm...I'm....I'm just saying it sounded like she was being unreasonable.

Wife: Don't call my mother a bitch. She is stressed out and dealing with a lot right now.

What just happened? I thought I was agreeing with her, I'm normally in the clear when I agree with her. This example is completely (ish) fabricated, but if it did happen, I'm sure a similar conversation could have taken place on the other side of that phone. Had my father-in-law or brother-in-law interjected in this hypothetical situation, my mother-in-law would have defended her daughter and turned on any "xy" chromosome carrier.

Family Feud

As I began this book, I denounced any expertise on any particular subject. However, I will argue that if I had to select a field of expertise it would be in family drama. I have enough experience both in my personal and professional life to justify specializing in this discipline.

Don't get me wrong, I don't want you to think I'm unique in my familiarity of drama. Rather, I'm aware of the abundance I have heard and witnessed on the subject. I believe fighting within any family is natural whether about dividing daily chores or mundane bickering. I also believe these disagreements don't end with your childhood. The jealousy, resentment and residual anger gets carried into adulthood.

The bond between a mother and daughter is a special one. It is, in my opinion one of the most complex relationships. It can be a beautiful, nurturing healthy connection where a parent will attempt to pass their values and beliefs to her child. When the daughter does not share those particular beliefs or when she has a conflicting personality, that is when a disconnect can occur.

We recently celebrated my grandmother's 90th birthday. Grandma is still in rocking shape; she is probably one of the toughest people I have met under four feet. This birthday party made me think of the women in my life. Looking back at past generations, women have seen a significant change in their roles which has led to a shift in the balance of households. Today's woman does not need to be bare foot and pregnant in the kitchen. Women can have fewer children, smaller families or no children at all. Women have a right to debate pro-choice/pro-life. They can attend school and focus on their professional careers. Women can be executive directors or CEO's of large agencies or corporations. They can be in same sex relationships and can choose to get married or not.

We're not just talking about a generation gap. We're talking about a huge shift in the women's movement. Women are recognized as individuals. They rise to the top of corporate ladders while balancing a personal life. The opportunities are endless when compared to previous generations. I think these options can lead to resentment and confusion. Some mothers may not understand because they were never provided with choices. Some mothers may feel they didn't have much of a say in the direction their life took.

As a result of these contrasts in lives, I often witness judgmental or ignorant passive-aggressive comments aimed at decisions they themselves would never have been faced with.

Sibling Rivalry

Another fun family feud fiasco lies among sibling rivalries. This common conflict typically starts at a young age when siblings fight for their parent's affection and attention. A reasonable level of sibling rivalry is a healthy way of expressing themselves and establishing boundaries. Parents are always comparing their children whether consciously or not. It may start with developing milestones, sleeping or eating patterns and often include behavioural aspects as early as infancy.

As siblings get older, the rivalry continues and is no longer limited to winning their parents acceptance. Siblings will often compare their relationships, the size of their home, their jobs or careers. They may even compare their interpretation of happiness (please note this is not limited to women. Men do this all the time, however for the purpose of Rule 3, we will focus on women).

My wife and I have a theory about back-to-back same gender siblings. If the age gap is not significant, there's a noticeable personality clash between siblings. My brother and I are 20 months apart. We couldn't be more dissimilar in physical appearance, personality traits, strengths and weaknesses. Our nieces are les then 3 years apart and are in the same boat as us. I challenge you to look into your family and social circle for more examples and discover it for yourself.

If mother/daughter relationships are unique special bonds and sibling rivalry are common among both genders, why am I spending a lot of time talking about them?

The reason I mention it, is because at some point you will be faced with certain pressures and expectations to choose sides. For no reason (well no apparent reason), you may be placed in the middle of a situation where you will be asked for feedback. Your comments may lead you down a strange path with a brand new set of obstacles. It will be difficult for you to remain neutral or unscathed. Sometimes you will have to take mental inventory, weigh out the pros and cons of engaging in what appears to be harmless looking traps because mother and daughters or siblings may unite quickly and turn on an outsider for having an opinion.

Friendly Fallout

Watching your girlfriend or spouse arguing with their BFF[12] is never a good situation. You can't expect to effectively choose sides but you may be expected to weigh in and be loyal. I caution you; although you may have no choice in the matter, you do have the liberty of carefully crafting your reply. Some friendships are long lasting (remember the second 'F' in BFF stands for forever), but there is a good chance this fight won't be. Your input and comments, if not handled with tact and diplomacy may echo forever.

Suddenly the comments you made out of devotion to your partner are being used against you by either your partner or her bestie. It's a no win situation.

---

12 BFF is a millennial overused acronym that stands for Best Friend Forever. Often used liberally and not meant literally (Urban Dictionary, n.d.).

Workplace Witch

Some female rivalries in the workplace are rooted in insecurities and jealousy. Such workplaces are predominately male driven, creating an environment that promotes female antagonisms. Competitive milieus where managerial positions are mostly held by men promote a system where women strive for positions and titles seldom awarded to female employees.

A setting is created where women are pinned against each other which often results in workplace aggression, gossip and rumours. Instead of celebrating each other's achievement they focus on their competitors flaws and attempt to justify their success. Women will attribute other's accomplishments to either looks or the ability to sleep their way to the top, while failing to acknowledge their skill level.

In order to not be thrown under the bus, I attempt to remain neutral and uninvolved. I believe women will rule the world one day. Hitching my wagon to the wrong horse could have catastrophic implications. Much like the butterfly effect, I understand that small decisions can have larger, life changing effects.

Fortunately for me, I work in a female dominated workplace. It's not surprising to see women in management roles and consequently, I deal with a lot less drama.

Schoolgirl Bully

Relational aggression is very common, ranging from elementary to high school. This form of aggression can be toxic for a learning environment and can impede social development. Typically, there is a pact leader who accepts only certain people within their clique. They will exclude and dislike people outside their social circle. These outsiders become subjected to isolation, ridicule or harassment.

The schoolyard aggressor can manipulate, intimidate or play mind games. This form of bullying can have life lasting effects such as anxiety, depression, or even suicide.

There's a study that found "members of groups run by aggressive girls appear to be caring and helpful towards each other however;

they also observe a higher level of intimacy and secret sharing in these groups. This closeness puts followers at risk because the aggressive child is privy to personal information that she can disclose. They also noted a higher level of exclusivity in groups run by relational aggressive girls. In other words, the followers usually have few other friends to turn to if they are rejected by the aggressive child; hence they continue to conform for fear of being isolated. They found a higher level of aggression within these groups" (Crick & Grotpeter, 1995).

How would anyone benefit from getting involved or attempting to dissuade a schoolyard bully? I believe men are more likely to engage in physical aggression while women seem more likely to partake in verbal aggression. Don't rack your brain on this one. Instead, go watch *Mean Girls* and ask yourself why you would inconvenience yourself with such social drama. Both genders experience aggression in different ways (Williams, Freland, Han, Campbell, & Kub, 2018). Women view their aggression as often coming from excessive stress and loss of control. Males on the other hand view it as an exercise in control of others brought by a challenge to their self-esteem and integrity.

The books and magazines articles I have read suggest women are more rational in their arguments, while other sources claim they are overly emotional. Some suggest women fight with intelligent and fair arguments while others suggest they are ruthless, calculated and cunning creatures. The words vengeful, resentful and begrudging were a re-occurring theme.

I was getting confused with the overwhelming and conflicting information on the internet. Some sources showed percentages that represent a decrease in the number of women who act out in an aggressive manner while other statistics indicated a rise in violence amongst women. I always felt statistics could be manipulated to reflect whatever you desired. After all, 98% of statistics are made up, 60 % of people know that. All statistics aside, what I know is this; there is something simplistic about the way men fight among men. There are normally two possible outcomes.

1. They get over it – men move on, potentially sharing a beer (not literally sharing one beer between both of them) or hugging it out (literally pressing their bodies together).

2. They stay out of each other's way. Most men don't feel the need to include everyone in their lives.

After an altercation, the situation is usually done with. There are few grudges, nary any gossip and minimal vengeful plans when compared with girls' interactions. At least that's what I understood based on my experienced and the very reliable people on Wiki How. The problem I have with the data are the contradictions and inaccurate comparisons between genders. Never mind comparing female aggression to males. Let's define girls from women.

Girls VS Women

It has been brought to my attention that like the some media sources, I've been guilty of using both nomenclatures interchangeably, despite significant differences. It's like comparing apples to oranges. There are distinctions and differences when we attempt to discriminate between girls and women. For this reason, I make great efforts to use the accurate terminology. While my obvious starting point focused on maturity, when I peeled back the layers, I realized there were differences beyond age and maturity.

I see girls as individuals characterized by emotional outbursts when their expectations are not met, reverting to childlike behaviours, including tantrums and fits. This misconduct may have worked on their parents and peers which is why they continue to behave this way.

I see Divas, expecting to be pampered and treated like a princesses. These royal pains often rely on others to take care of them, solve their problems, and accomplish undesired chores or mundane day to day tasks. These drama queens value superficialities such as property, possessions and physical appearances. Perhaps as a result of being objectified by others, they no longer respect their bodies and resort to using it as currency or a weapon to get what they want. They will wear provocative outfits and behave inappropriately in order to feel sexy and get attention. These are the same people who will not hesitate to slut shame others for engaging in similar attention-seeking ploys.

Women on the other hand, tend to not shy away or back down from obstacles or challenges. Rather, they arm themselves with assertiveness to tackle difficult situations or face adversity. They choose self-reliance, solving problems independently. Women don't need to dress in a revealing fashion to look sexy. A woman dresses for herself and not others. Women are confident and secure enough to stand up for their beliefs. They will support one another instead of participating in idle talks or gossip about the affairs of another.

The complexity of female to female interactions is what solidifies rules 3. Since we don't know what to expect, it's not safe for anyone to be interfering. Because certain females have established their ability to be mean and cruel with one another, there's no reason for men to poke their nose and attempt to rectify the situation. All you are doing is drawing attention to yourself. Suddenly you could have two people upset with you, recruiting others, influencing them to exclude you while holding a grudge.

I once heard a female stand-up comedian talking about world peace. She mentioned that there would be no war if the president of the United States of America was female (I hope she meant woman and not girl).

Her statement was based on the belief that women, especially mothers, are more compassionate and reasonable when making decisions. She also mentioned that they think big picture and consider long-term consequences without allowing ego to clout their judgement.

While I don't deny the United States would benefit from female leadership (especially given the Dorito dusted farce they are dealing with now), I do disagree with her premise. I believe her intended statement was that war would be prevented if all leaders of the world were rational women, not just the United States of America.

I don't agree or disagree with this theory. It's amusing to consider it. Imagine if the leaders of the world were all overgrown girls; adult girls with world-altering decision-making abilities. I would hate to be the world leader who gets caught up in the web of a mean girl. She would not only be subjected to gossip and secret-sharing but her adversary would have a nation's resource at hand. She would have the country's defense and arsenal at her disposal to execute her revenge.

CONCLUSION

"When people agree with me I always
feel that I must be wrong."
— Oscar Wilde

I hope you've enjoyed reading this book as much as I've enjoyed writing it. My intent was not for you to identify people in your life who are guilty of committing those infractions as you read each chapter. If this were the goal, I would have provided a sheet of penis stickers with this book for you to distribute to people as you see fit. It was also not my intention to convince you I'm not guilty of these violations. There are so many different behaviours that lead to being a dick. Too many to list in this book. I feel like I have covered most categories, however as I am wrapping things up, I feel there are a few additional groups worth mentioning.

Over-Exaggerators

I instantly get peeved when I hear the gross exaggerations in the limited vocabulary of our millennials. A great way to ruffle my feathers is by using FML[13] when describing menial problems. Clearly this is a violation of Rule 2.

---

13   FML = Fuck My Life (Urban Dictionary, n.d.)

Another eye-roll inducing turn of phrase is "I almost died." This term is almost always used to describe a non-lethal or non-fatal situation. It is used when death was not even remotely imminent.

OMG, TMI, Don't be dick! Do not use shorthand during face to face conversations.

The last millennial expression that gets under my skin is when people use the word 'literally[14]' to describe a figurative topic or obvious situation.

"I literally told you a bazillion times."

...really? Literally a bazillion times? That's not even a real number Dick! Therefore, there is no way you could have been exact, precise or truthful. You could not have told me anything exactly, precisely or directly a bazillion times.

I remember someone telling me she used this term when she was 'super serious' about a topic. However, given the ridiculousness of that one word used incorrectly, I would only focus on that exaggeration rather than the message. I could never bring myself to use it the way millennials do.

"I had to work this morning, so I woke up at 6 am, I almost died... literally. FML".

I am guilty of being a dick (Constant Corrector) when faced with those statements. Why do Millennials use such over-exaggerations (← Askhole statement)? I know I've picked on Millennials a lot throughout this book. Sorry, not sorry[15]. Deal with it. The Silent Generation was harsh towards the Baby Boomers who in turn would chastise Generation X for their ethics and values. As a lost generation stuck between Gen X and Millennials[16], it is our turn to instill ruthless judgement on the next generation ready to take over and fuck up the world.

14 Literally means in a literal sense or manner (Merriam-Webster, 2021) or used to describe something that actually happened or exists (Urban Dictionary, n.d.). It is one of the most overused words in modern society (Urban Dictionary, n.d.).

15 Sorry not sorry is typically used to signified that the speaker does not care whether their behavior emotionally upset someone else (Urban Dictionary, n.d.).

16 Xennials – is the new term for the microgeneration of people born between 1977 and 1983 (Urban Dictionary, n.d.). "As an older millennial I always resented being lumped in with this group. You see, we came of age before social media and iphones, we were raised in an analog world, and dropped into a digital universe. We are xennials" (MrsPartridge, 2017)

Why ask Why?

Another noteworthy rule two violator are those who insist on asking why. In my opinion, this is one of the worst questions someone can ask. Not only is it a waste of time, but it comes off as accusatory. It's a judgmental line of questioning that automatically puts me on the defense.

It's good to ask questions, as its part of active listening and being an effective communicator. We use open and closed ended questions in order to gain information, clarification or to learn more on a particular subject. Asking "why" however is a good way to shut down communication.

My wife is the queen of asking why. She'll use a why statement when the answer is plain and evident. She'll even ask why when the answer is irrelevant. I remember preparing to bake a desert for a work pot luck. I was studying a recipe card and gathering ingredients. My wife, Your Highness of Whyness, was quick to inquire.

Wife: I'm headed to the store, do you need anything?

Me: (reading the recipe card) Yeah, I'll need some icing sugar and some butter.

Wife: why?

Me: Because I use it to shave!

What a silly question. It leads me to believe that if she's not satisfied with the answer she won't honour my request.

"Can I have my epipen?"

"Why?"

No matter what the answer is to the "why" the other person will most likely comply so why ask why?

Cat Lovers

What the fuck (Not WTF)? We all know cats are the biggest dicks in the animal kingdom. They do what they want whenever they want. Why do we embrace an animal that stands in its own toilet and then walks all over your bed, couch and table? I know some of you Cat People are lying to yourself, saying not my cat. But yes, your cat too! Celebrating these furry feline fece-footed fucks just enables them to become bigger dicks, making you a dick by proxy.

Hipsters

I'm not talking about the Hipsters from the 30's who were into Jazz. These people were cool cats (no the same cats as previously mentioned). I am talking about the subculture who are into indi-rock, wear scarves out of season and have an ironic attitude about everything. I'm referring to the individuals who are anti-establishment, organic, vegan, holistic people who are into retro and vintage fads.

These Hipsters are the type of sarcastic people who try too hard to be unique and express their strong opinions towards popular trends. The irony of it all, is that being a hipster is a popular trend, dick! The Hipster characteristics fall under many rule 2 behaviours.

I was recently introduced as a hipster by a young client to her mother. I was appalled to be labelled as a member of this counter-culture. Just because I have a beard and wear plaid does not make me a hipster. A co-worker pointed out that I do hate popular culture and enjoy non-conventional music, craft beers and tattoos. I had to remind everyone that I hate a lot of things, not ironically, but genuinely. I don't have the time, energy or patience to go out of my way to embrace anti-establishment behaviours. I'm asshole, but not a dick.

Asinine Advertisers

I sure hope I'm not the only person who gets annoyed with decals and stickers on vehicles. Don't get me wrong, if you root for a sports team or are promoting a service or product this section does not apply to you.

I get particularly annoyed with parents who think anyone gives a shit if their child is an honour roll student. In a generation of participation ribbons, who is not on the honour roll? Congrats mom and dad, you just provided bullies with a location to find nerds.

Stick finger family? Why? (That's right! I am annoyed enough to ask why). Congrats mom and dad, you just assisted local pedophiles to zone in on the whereabouts of minors. Judging by the stickers on the back of your Caravan there are at least 3 targets (specifically 2 boys and 1 girl).

Baby on board. I feel this decal is an old relic. I was told it was used to alert emergency medical technicians to look for an infant at the scene of accident. I can only assume that this decal pre-dated the mandatory laws involving car seats. Nowadays you don't have to be a mathmagician to figure out the equation. 1 car accident, plus 1 car seat may equate to a potential child involved.

Also, I refuse to believe this sign prevents car accidents. I don't believe people with road rage, who are ready to engage you in a game of bumper tag will be discouraged by a diamond shape deterrent.

A new source of annoyance in the decal world are the "Fuck Cancer" signs emblazoned on the windshield of vehicles. I'm not sure this statement is necessary.

Some level of annoyance is also reserved for the "Support the Troops" bumper stickers. Do we need to advertise that we are hoping our brave soldiers come back alive?

Could you imagine if someone inverted the emphasis on those decals?

- Support Cancer
- Fuck the troops

Be careful where you park you Prius. My point is no one is going out of their way to refute these statements. Plastering them on your car just seems redundant. Why not include these:

- Rape is bad
- Boo Arson!
- Yeah Sunshine
- Open Bar – Woohooo

Mr. Meathead

You know who you are. If you're looking around the gym and can't find them, look at the person staring back at you in the mirror, that grunting mesomorph who regularly skips leg day. The guy who walks with that "after workout pump" all day long, clutching a gallon jug, workout powders, creatine and whatever else causes bacne, rage and shrunken testicles.

I'm referring to this one particular type of individual. Every time I'm at the gym he is talking about his working out instead or exercising. This guy who has over developed traps and no neck. His muscles have muscles. The big red flag for me was his workout routine. Every time I spotted him at the gym, I was able to complete cardio, my workout and my shower while this guy would fail to complete even a single set. He seldom does any actual exercise, yet he looks like he's a WWE pro wrestler. He reminds me of this guy I met at a bar during a St. Paddy's day celebration.

My buddy and I attend a pub in the Irish Village on the morning of St. Paddy's day to meet up with a few friends. One girl we met up with had brought her new boyfriend. He was not especially large. He was short but built and walked like he was 8 feet wide. By the time we had our second pitcher of beer he was peacocking and trying to start some shit with my buddy. My friend just happened to be the smallest guy in the bar. In retrospect I should have let Smalls (that's what I call him) knock him on his ass, but I was trying to keep the peace and remain civilized. I interjected and this is how it went down (I literally stooped down to his level).

Me: What are we doing here? (I have since learned that I use this term often when frustrated or irritated and it annoys my spouse significantly)

I stepped in between them, forcing my face to be uncomfortably close to his.

Me: We just want to grab some drinks and catch the game.

Meathead: Yeah Bro, I got no beef with you. Your bud needs to shut his mouth or I'll shut it for him.

Me: Okay, I'm just letting you know that when that happens it will be my turn to shut some mouths.

Meathead: No Bro! I've always respected you (he met me an hour ago). It is him that I have never been able to tolerate (he met him an hour ago).

Meathead: I like you bro, out of respect to you I won't do anything.

By the next pitcher of beer I had to visit the men's room to empty the tank. I have the bladder of an infant. I came back to witness the Napoleon Neanderthal shoving my buddy and threatening him.

Meathead: Come at me Bro.

I don't quite remember the monolog I performed because it was awhile back and it was alcohol induced. I do remember grabbing the guy by the face to push him away. I also remember pointing out his douchy behaviour which included but was not limited to him checking himself out in every reflective surface and flexing for the waitress. I remember finishing my speech by letting him know he was not worth my energy or effort today. There were too many drinking hours left and we were off to celebrate instead of wasting another minute with this ass clown. We walked away while everyone watched us. We were halfway out of the bar when I realized I had left my coat at the table.

I would have left my jacket behind but it had my wallet, keys and phone. I returned to the group, walk of shame style. Everyone was still reacting and discussing what just took place. Mr. Meathead must have been surprised because he flinched when I reached for my coat. As I headed out I heard him mutter "you better walk away." What a dick (no balls though). It took everything I had not to come back again and show him how hard a muscle meathead falls.

This journey was longer than I originally anticipated. Veering off on a few tangents, but I'm hoping I didn't lose people when I ventured off the path and got caught up in my rants. I was hoping to act as a Sherpa, by providing some insight and perspective. People don't have to agree with everything that was said in this book. In fact, I would be concerned if they did. My objective was not to convert everyone and be rid of all dicks. I just wanted to help people do an inventory of their communicating styles and determine if they're adding or taking away from conversations, while highlighting the importance of being an effective communicator.

I knew I was not the first person to come up with this concept. While writing this book I discovered Wheaton's Law[17]. An idea expressed at the Penny Arcade Expo in 2007 by Will Wheaton III (the third? Oooh la la). He made his own declaration of this rule in relation to gaming, in an attempt to discourage cyber bullying. Now, I'm not a savvy lad when it comes to the internet world nor am I aware of what is currently trending, but apparently since 2009, people have been adopting this concept as the rule of the internet. Beyond the internet world, this concept has branched out and reached other levels of people's lives[18].

On his birthday, William Wheaton the Third (damn, that's a bad ass name) has expressed that as a gift, he would like for this day to be known as "Don't be a Dick Day" (Wheaton, n.d.). This day of course just happens to fall exactly on my old man's birthday. Coincidence, I think not. I could think of no more reason for this rule to be in effect. Thanks, Will.

I take solace in knowing I'm not the only one out there who believes we should not be dicks. I hum the chorus of "Don't be a Dick" by 'Bowling for Soup' as I think of the endless applications of this rule. Don't be a Dick is a concept that just makes sense to me. It discourages behaviours that are prone to hinder healthy dialogues between people while promoting active listening. I feel there is a growing amount of evidence that indicates our society is doomed when it comes to communication. We have developed various ways to avoid direct human interactions through social media and have lost the ability to be assertive. It's time to take a technological step back, go back to the basics and learn how to talk to one another, and listen. Thank you and Don't be a Dick.

---

17 Wheaton's Law is an internet axiom which states "Don't be a dick." It was originally used in the context of sportsmanship in online gaming but its scope was eventually expanded to apply to life in general (Wheaton's Law, 2007).

18 Whether you're dealing with your opposing counsel, a colleague at your firm or any other professional, Wheaton's Law should always apply. "You would think Wheaton's Law should be standard practice for all lawyers, but the horde of horror stories paints a different picture. There are lawyers who think less of anyone who is not a lawyer. And there are the ones who procrastinate on their work before dumping it on an associate — giving them a day to complete a project that requires a week. Then there are the lawyers who get into screaming matches during depositions" (Carver, n.d.).

ACKNOWLEDGEMENT

"Don't cry because it is over.
Smile because it happened."
— Dr. Suess

A little thanks goes a long way. I would like to take some time to recognize some of the people whose efforts and inspiration have made this book possible.

MJ, my wife, you have had infinite patience with me. You've tolerated and supported me through this process, and just in general. Thank you for the many cheeseburgers we shared. You've also participated and tolerated countless communication breakdowns which have been a source of inspiration throughout this book.

My darling daughter, Rosabelle. You are our hope. You are the motivation for me to become a better, more effective communicator. Your mother and I continue to practice this concept to teach you assertiveness and remain inspired to lead you by example for fear that you may turn out to be a dick.

Tracy Handy, you've been my sounding board while I wrote this book. Every week I got to try out my material with you. You've rewarded me with your laughter and your disagreeing head shakes. While you did not approve of me bashing the millennials you still proofread my first draft. Thank you for helping me with grammar and nonsense writing.

Jill Hodgson, despite balancing work, school and parenting, you've also managed to find some time editing the dyslexic jumble of words I strung together. You've exercised your Di Vinci skills in deciphering the rants of a Frenchman and making it legible for everyone. I'm forever grateful for the energy you put in this project.

Special acknowledgment to Natasha Dingwall, who has enlightened me on the differences between women and girls, and encouraged me not to make general statements based on gender (despite my rants in rule #3). You've reminded me that dicks are not male specific, they exist in both genders.

Father Jason Pollick, merci. Your brilliant sermons and keen way of delivering your messages remains with me forever.

A special shout out to Joe Random, who has been used throughout the book. Thanks for always being there.

I want to thank the ladies of Taco Tuesday, Chantal and Lark. You've witness our many tirades. Your place of work was the birth place of this concept.

I would like to recognize Gina Dragone Photography. I am not a photogenic person, so I am grateful for this usable shot, which by the way looks way better without my family cropped out of it.

Posthumous acknowledgement to Captain Cliché. RIP

I would like to raise a glass (of scotch, but not too peaty) to a local celebrity who is no stranger to performing on air and in front of a crowd. Dan Allaire, you are a standup guy. Your personality can lift spirits and fill a room with laughter. Thank you for trying something new, and writing my forward. Who knows, perhaps one day I will write yours. Cheers!

To all the Dicks out there, from all walks of life, thanks you! This book would not exist without you. Without your annoyance, ignorance and frustrating ways, I would not have put pen to paper (that's right, I literally put pen to paper) and created this book.

Last but not lease, Mark Snelgrove. Thank you for being the mid-wife of creativity and helping me deliver this book. Your wisdom, experience and morally grey attitude served as the catalyst that help transform this simple lunch time rant, to an actual book.

REFERENCES

Carver, R. (n.d.). *Nothing but the Ruth! Wheaton's Law*. Retrieved from Attorney At Work.

Crick, N. R., & Grotpeter, J. K. (1995). Relational Aggression, Gender and Social-Psychological Adjustment. *Child Development, vol. 66(3)*, 710-722.

Crowe, C. (Director). (1982). *Fast Time at Ridgemount High* [Motion Picture].

First, Second, and Third World. (2021). Retrieved from One World - Nations Online: https://www.nationsonline.org/oneworld/third_world_countries.htm

Kuhn, M. (2008). *Bro Code: Barney Stinson*. New York: Fireside.

Merriam-Webster. (2021). Retrieved from Merriam-Webster: www.merriam-webster.com

MrsPartridge. (2017, July 19). Retrieved from Urband Dictionary: https://www.urbandictionary.com/define.php?term=xennial

Noel, A., & Cedilo, A. (2010). *Mafia Inc.: The Long, Bloody Reign or Canada's Sicilian Clan*. Quebec: Random House.

Oxford Languages. (2021). Retrieved from Oxford Languages: www.oxforddictionaries.com

Ozier, A. (n.d.). Retrieved from Cyber Bullying: https://www.sutori.com/story/cyber-bullying--9EQCr1ZGmyjSMRki7TnprJ9E

Pollock, R. J. (2018). *Dictionary of Symbols*. Retrieved from www.dictionaryofsymbols.blogspot.ca

Seligman, M. (2002). *Authentic Happiness: Using the New Positive Psychology to Realize Your Potential for Lasting Fulfillment*. New York: Free Press.

Slang. (n.d.). Retrieved from Slang: www.slang.org

Urban Dictionary. (n.d.). Retrieved from www.urbandictionary.com

Wheaton, W. (n.d.). Retrieved from Don't Be a Dick Day: https://dontbeadickday.com/

Wheaton's Law. (2007). Retrieved from Know Your Meme: https://knowyourmeme.com/memes/wheatons-law

Williams, J., Freland, N., Han, H.-R., Campbell, J., & Kub, J. (2018). Relational Aggression and Adverse Psychosocial and Physical Health Symptoms Among Urban Adolescents. *US National Library of Medicine National Institutes of Health.*

Winch, G. (2011, July 15). *How to Deal with Chronic Complainers.* Retrieved from Psychology Today: https://www.psychologytoday.com/ca/blog/the-squeaky-wheel/201107/how-deal-chronic-complainers